GW00322489

FIRST PONY

FIRST PONY

Toni Webber

WARD LOCK LIMITED · LONDON

First published in Great Britain in 1986
by Ward Lock Limited, 8 Clifford Street,
London W1X 1RB, an Egmont Company.

Line drawings by Kevin Maddison

Photographs by Peter Loughran
The publishers would like to thank Radnage House Riding School, Radnage Bucks for their help with the pictures on p. 10 and p. 30.

Text set in Palatino
by J & L Composition Ltd, Filey, N. Yorks

Printed and bound in Italy
by Sagdos

British Library Cataloguing in Publication Data

Webber, Toni
First pony book.
1. Ponies——Juvenile literature 2. Horsemanship —Juvenile literature
I. Title
798.2 SF315

ISBN 0-7063-6434-1

Contents

For Charlotte and *her* succession of ponies – Hannibal, Smokey Joe, Bowsy and Minnie – and for Katie, Penny and Lucy and *theirs* – Dusty, Rocky, Snowy, Tammy, Toby, Bowsy, Dillon, Sandy, Andy Pandy, Brandy, Solly, Andy and, of course, Gumboots.

Introduction

Once upon a time – seventy years ago or more – there were people around who were worried that riding as a leisure activity would die out. They were concerned that the art of horsemanship would be practised by a mere handful of enthusiasts and that Britain's unique collection of indigenous pony breeds would dwindle to near extinction. As more and more working horses were replaced by machines, it must have seemed increasingly likely that their prophecies would come true.

They had reckoned, however, without the fervour and devotion that horses and ponies arouse in people of all ages – and particularly in small girls. Most families with young daughters are only too aware of the symptoms: the eagle eyes that can spot ponies five fields off as the family car speeds along a country road, the posters of ponies obliterating the bedroom walls, the imaginary pony living in the corner of the outhouse or garage and, overlying everything else, the incessant nagging to be allowed to have riding lessons or, better still, to replace the imaginary pony with a real, live, flesh-and-blood one.

In recent years, riding has continued to grow in popularity and the number of people who ride or own horses can be numbered in hundreds of thousands. Every week, their ranks are joined by families who have succumbed to the persistence of their children, as yet another newcomer takes her first steps on the back of a horse.

This book is for those who are contemplating buying a pony and is intended for both parents and children. The first, no doubt, are facing the prospect with trepidation, the second with dauntless enthusiasm.

It may comfort the parents to know that almost everyone buying a new horse or pony – unless they are very young – feels some anxiety about their new purchase. Most new buyers ask themselves – when the cheque is written and the horse delivered – whether they have done the right thing. What question did they forget to ask? Is this pony or horse everything it seems to be? Is it absolutely safe in traffic? Is that small scar on the near fetlock as trivial as the vet claims?

New owners have a whole host of further worries to concern them. Even a small pony is a bigger animal than any they have had to cope with before. Its needs are quite different from a dog's or a cat's. It is, in short, a major responsibility.

The aim of this book is to prepare the ground for first-time owners. It tells the reader how to set about finding a suitable pony and how to look after it once it has been acquired. The information is aimed primarily at the pony's younger owner but a wise parent will brush up on the facts, too, because ultimately the responsibility must fall on an adult who also, of course, pays the bills.

Fortunately, a first pony – one that lives out all the year round and takes part in a limited number of Pony Club and other activities – need not be a very expensive possession, but it would be foolish to expect a child's average weekly pocket money to cover all the costs. It is also likely to be demanding of both time and attention and, for everyone's sake, it is just as well to be prepared.

Once ventured into, pony-owning is very rewarding. It surprises parents sometimes to find how attached they become to their child's pride and joy. Mothers trudge happily for miles with pony and rider on the end of a lead-rope, and even the mundane tasks of mucking out or cleaning tack can actually be good fun. Later on, of course, it is possible to spend almost all one's spare time doing things with horses, but that – for the moment at least – is quite another story.

Toni Webber

CHAPTER 1
Learning to ride

It is a matter of choice which you do first: learn to ride, or get your own pony. If you are wise, you will learn to ride first. Then you can enjoy your pony to the full once you have acquired him. Some families, however, like the idea of having the pony available for a child to learn on. But this works on the whole only when other members of the family know how to look after a pony, or when you know of someone else – the daughter, say, of a knowledgeable friend – who can help to keep the pony regularly exercised and properly cared for.

Nevertheless, there are situations where it would be madness not to buy the pony first; such as when the perfect schoolmaster becomes available and, unless you jump in quickly, the pony will go to another child. Even then, the parents must be able to keep him, virtually as a pet, during the months, or even a year or two, before his new young owner is ready to cope with him all by herself.

Most of you, no doubt, will learn to ride first. This is best done at a reputable riding school, preferably one which has an indoor school for training sessions but which also takes its pupils hacking from time to time. There is almost certainly one in your area, and if you have a choice ask around before you ring up for an appointment. Word-of-mouth recommendation is important.

Equally important, you and your parents should pay a visit to the school before booking a lesson. Your visit should include a tour of the stables so that you can see the conditions in which the ponies are kept. Loose boxes should be light and airy, with good thick beds of straw or shavings and no sign of stale droppings. The stables need not be sparkling with new paint (better that the school should spend more on good-quality food for the ponies than on window-dressing to impress clients) but they should have an air of cleanliness and caring about them. The tack room should be tidy, with the saddles and bridles clean and well-kept, and the food store should be dry, the floor swept and the feed kept in vermin-proof bins.

Most revealing of all are the ponies themselves. Contented, well-fed ponies take an interest in the things going on around them and your visit (unless, of course, it is at feeding time) should bring heads peering over stable doors, ears pricked and eyes bright and alert.

Before finishing your tour of the stables, you should look at the muck-heap. A conscientious owner of a well-kept stable will also have a well-kept muck-heap. This means one that is properly squared off with a flat top and no soiled straw or old dung scattered in the yard.

Ask if you can sit in on a lesson. If the instructor has a recognized teaching qualification (in the UK this is a British Horse Society Assistant Instructor's (BHSAI) certificate), it does not, of course, mean that she is necessarily a good instructor; but it does ensure that the standards of riding she teaches and the methods she uses are recognized. Only observation will give you a hint as to how skilful she is and how enjoyable she manages to make her lessons. A good instructor should build up an understanding between herself and her pupils, so study the reactions of the children taking part in the lesson you are watching. Do they respond well to her orders, does she joke with them, does she vary the tone of her voice according to which child she has to correct or give orders to? Does she shout too much, or not enough? And if they do something wrong, does she pick it up quickly and make certain that the fault is corrected?

When you are satisfied with all that you have seen, then is the time to book a lesson or, more probably, a series of lessons.

The complete beginner will almost certainly have the first one or two lessons on the lunge. This means that the instructor holds the pony on a long rein, while pony and pupil circle around her. From this distance, she can observe the rider's position in the saddle and the way the reins are being held. She can give instructions and observe how they are carried out. And all the time, the beginner knows that the pony cannot run away, so she can concentrate on riding correctly.

Once the instructor is satisfied with the pupil's progress, the lunge rein will be put away and pupil and pony can join a regular class.

This chapter covers much of what you will be taught by your instructor. It is not a substitute for a good teacher, but it will help you to remember what you have been taught.

THE FIRST LESSONS

Approaching the pony

One of the most important lessons you learn when you first start to ride is how to go up to a pony. A pony's natural instinct, if something frightens him, is to run away. However, they are, or should be, taught to trust human beings, so that they know that when humans are around there is no need to feel afraid. Young ponies may react quite sharply to something new although after a while, especially when they see that the human being is calm and unafraid, they forget their own fear. Wise, experienced ponies take most things in their stride, and these are the sort of ponies that should be ridden by beginners.

Nevertheless, you owe it to the pony, however old and wise, to treat him sensibly. Approach him from the front so that he can see you coming, and let your movements be unhurried. You may be eager to sit on his back for the first time, but spare a moment to stroke his nose or neck and to say 'Hello'. Your voice, in fact, is a very useful aid and it is surprising how often beginners – and indeed more experienced riders – forget that a conversation helps to build up trust between rider and pony.

Never rush up to the pony, especially from behind. At best, you might make him jump. At worst, he could kick out, and a kick from a pony can be very painful.

Mounting and dismounting

First check that the saddle girth is tight enough to prevent the saddle from slipping round when you put your weight in the stirrup. See that the stirrup-irons are down on both sides. You can adjust the leathers approximately to the correct length before mounting by placing the knuckles of your right hand on the stirrup-bar and altering the leathers until the bottom of the stirrup-iron reaches your armpit.

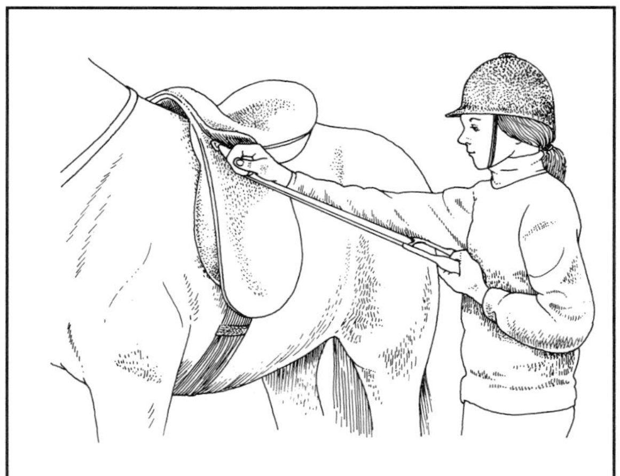

Checking the length of your stirrup-leathers before mounting.

The correct side from which to get on is, by tradition, the pony's left side, known as the *near side.* Stand by the pony's shoulder, take the rein by the buckle in your right hand and draw up the slack. Grasp both sides of the rein in your left hand at a point where the hand can rest lightly on the withers just in front of the saddle, and toss the loop of the rein over to the far side, known as the *off side.* Now, facing the pony's tail, put your left foot in the stirrup-iron and grasp the back of the saddle with the right hand. Spring upwards off your right foot, press the ball of the left foot down into the stirrup-iron, and swivel round as you do so, taking care that your toe does not dig the pony in the ribs. Straighten

Always visit a riding school before you arrange to have lessons there. Here, young riders line up while their instructor checks each pony in turn.

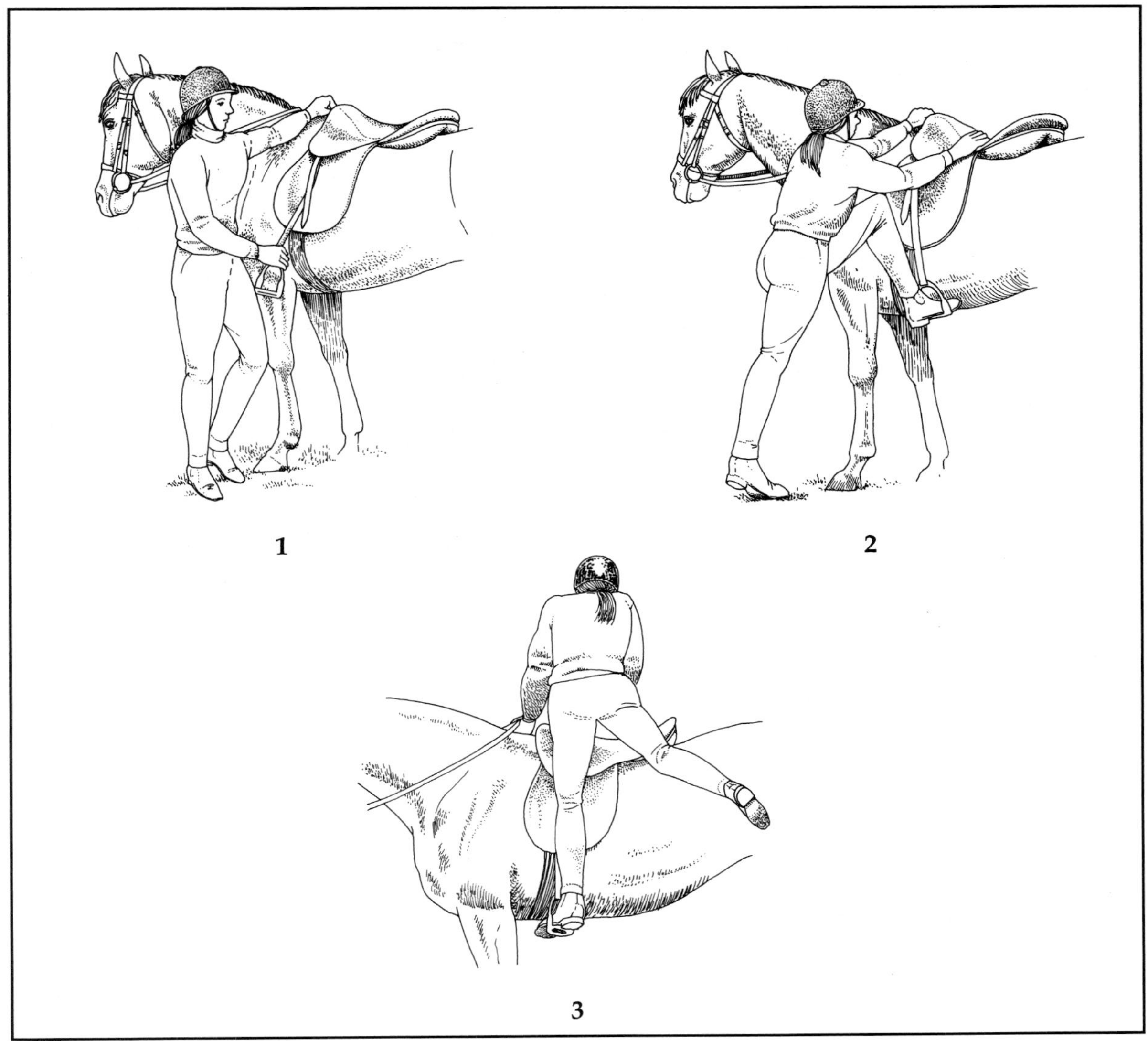

1 Preparing to mount. Stand facing the rear of the horse and gather up the reins in your left hand. **2** Place your left foot in the stirrup-iron and grasp the back of the saddle with your right hand. **3** Press down in the stirrup-iron and swing your free leg over the back of the saddle.

your knees and swing the right leg over the saddle without brushing the pony's loins, then lower yourself gently into the saddle. Place your right foot in the stirrup-iron and take up the reins in both hands.

The process of mounting should be as fluid and easy as possible, aimed at giving the pony the least discomfort. Try not to thump into the saddle, and make the time when all your weight is on one side as short as possible.

Dismounting is easier. Place your reins in your left hand and take both feet out of the stirrup-irons. Hold the pommel of the saddle with your right hand and swing your right leg over the saddle and slide to the ground, landing by the pony's shoulder. You should bend your knees on landing to absorb the jar. Take hold of the reins near the bit and stand by your pony's head.

If you have a whip, this should be held in the left hand, with the reins, for both mounting and dismounting. It is useful to practise these movements on both sides of the pony. In due course, when you start taking part in gymkhanas and other competitions, it saves time if you can mount or dismount with equal fluency from either side.

Your seat

Sit in the centre, or lowest part, of the saddle with your hips square and your back straight. Look towards the front over your pony's ears. Feel that your seat bones are in contact with the saddle. Nevertheless, to start with, it is important that you should feel comfortable.

A good position is one in which an imaginary line, at right angles to the ground, passes through your ear, shoulder, hip and the back of your heel.

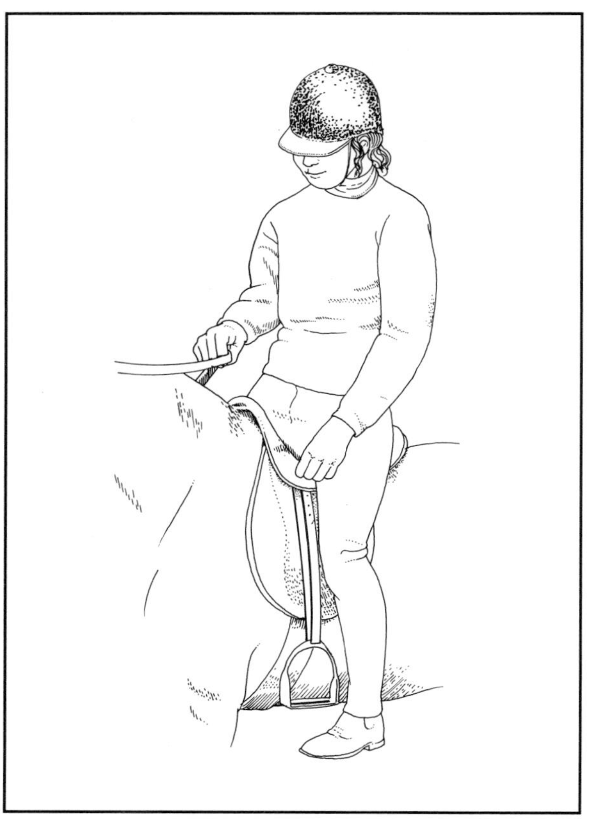

The stirrup-leathers are the correct length if the bottom of the stirrup-iron is level with your ankle bone.

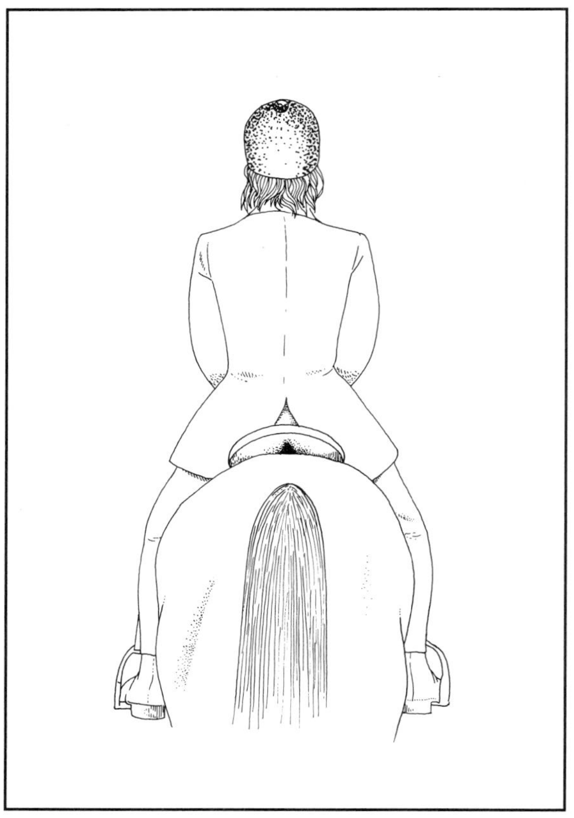

Always sit square in the saddle.

Before moving off, make certain that the stirrup-leathers are adjusted correctly. Take both feet out of the stirrups and let your legs hang down in a relaxed way. Your stirrup-leathers are the correct length if the bars of the irons are level with your ankle bones.

Beginners often complain that their leathers are too long, and shorter stirrups certainly give the illusion of greater security and better balance. As your riding improves, however, you will find that you need longer leathers to make your lower leg more effective. Short leathers tend to push you too far back in the

Holding the reins

Pick up the reins in both hands so that each side passes directly from the bit between the little and third finger, across the palm and out over the index finger, turning your wrists so that the thumbs are on top. Take up enough rein to maintain a light contact with the pony's mouth and allow the loop of spare rein to hang down on the near side. The elbows should be bent sufficiently to form a straight line along the forearm, wrists, hands and rein to the bit, whether it is viewed from above or from the side.

In a good position, an imaginary line, at right-angles to the ground, should pass through your ear, shoulder, hip and the back of your heel.

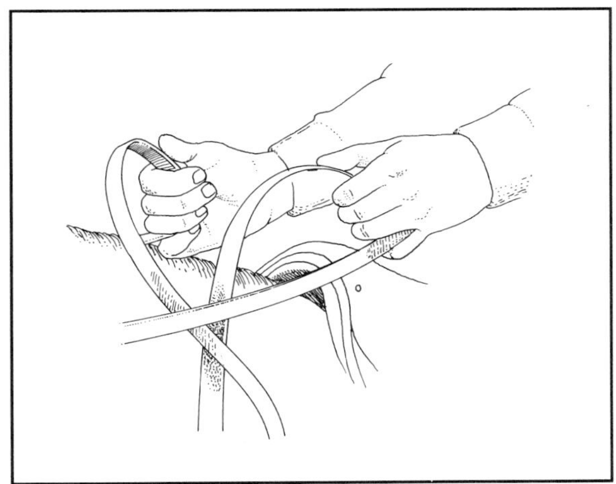

The correct way to hold the reins.

The rein and the fore-arm should form a straight line

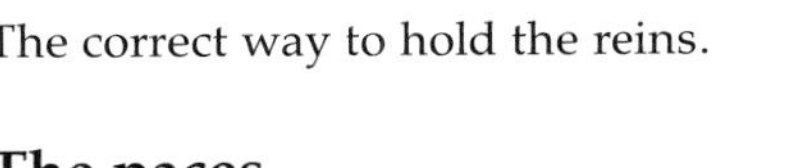

The paces

The pony's movements are known as the paces. Each pace has its own sequence of footfalls (see drawing overleaf) and a special term is used to describe it. The **walk** in which the four feet follow one another in turn, is called four-time. The **trot**, in which one diagonal pair of feet hits the ground together, followed by the other pair, is a pace of two-time. The **canter** has three beats, one diagonal pair coming to the ground together, and is known as three-time. In the **gallop**, although it is an extension of the canter, the diagonal pair of legs split slightly into separate footfalls so the gallop is termed a four-time pace.

The paces and your position

The walk Your seat at the walk is the same as when the pony is standing still, except that

Always present a titbit to a pony on the flat of your hand. Even the best of ponies can mistake your finger for something good to eat.

Opposite: A kind pony is essential for a young rider. This rider has complete confidence in her mount, yet her legs barely reach the bottom of the saddle flap.

your body moves slightly at the waist and hips in time with the pony's movement. A pony's head and neck nods rhythmically as he walks and you, in turn, follow the rhythm with your elbows and shoulders. All the time, you should aim at keeping an even, light contact with the pony's mouth. Unless you let your hands give with the movement, you will confuse the pony by pulling him repeatedly in the mouth.

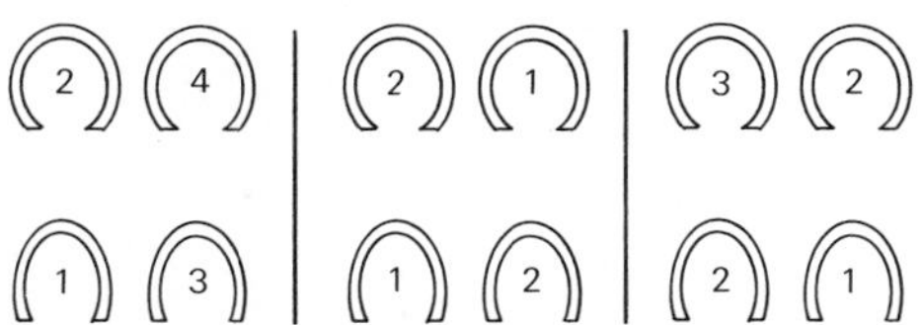

Sequence of footfalls. **Left** The walk (four-time). **Centre** The trot (two-time). **Right** The canter (three-time), shown here for a canter to the left. The diagonals are reversed for a canter to the right.

The trot This is the pace that most beginners dread, usually because they have heard how difficult it is from other learners who have already been through the mill. In fact, like so many other aspects of learning to ride, the rising trot is a matter of practice, and it is intended to keep rider and pony balanced and in harmony.

When a horse trots, he moves his two diagonal pairs of legs alternately. The action is bouncy and, at first, you will no doubt feel that you are being joggled right out of the saddle. To compensate for the bounciness and to make the pony feel comfortable at the trot with someone on his back, the rider rises out of the saddle as one pair of legs comes to the ground, and returns to the saddle in time with the other pair.

At first, you will probably find that by keeping one hand on the pommel of the saddle, you can push yourself up in time with

CHILDREN'S WORLD

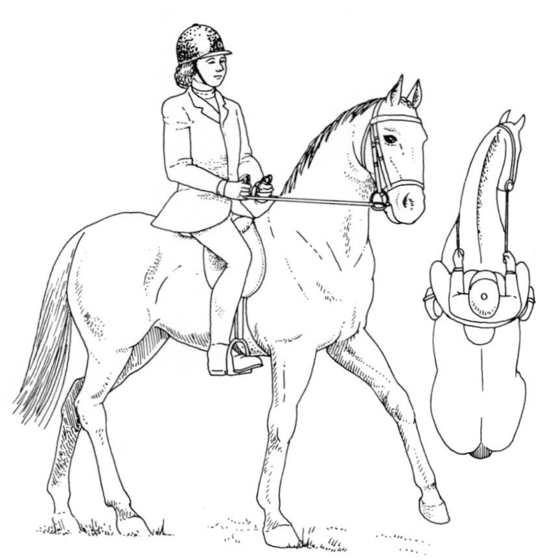

Turning right. Feel the right rein and relax the left sufficiently for the pony to be able to bend his neck as he turns.

Turning left. Use the opposite aids. Always remember that once the pony has obeyed your signal, you should stop applying that particular aid.

The rising trot, right diagonal, rider sitting.

The canter, with the rider sitting deep in the saddle.

the pony's movements. To start with, you will also tend to hollow your back and stick out your tummy. As you grow more proficient, however, you will no longer need the steadying hand and you will be able to keep your back straight. A slight forward movement of the upper body, from the hips, is necessary to keep you balanced, but the weight on your stirrup-irons should remain the same and your lower legs should stay as still as possible.

Once you have mastered the rising trot, remember to change the diagonal occasionally. This means that you miss a beat: for example, if you are sitting in the saddle when the horse's off-fore (front right) and near-hind (back left) legs come to the ground, you are on the *right diagonal;* if you sit for two beats then rise again, you will return to the saddle when the opposite pair of legs come to the ground, and you are on the *left diagonal*. This variation from time to time is kinder to the pony, especially if you are doing a great deal of trotting.

The canter This is a much easier pace for the rider to cope with than the trot. At a canter, a horse's stride has three beats, and you should stay in the saddle all the time. Try to keep your body supple and your shoulder and elbow joints mobile in order to absorb the beats and the movements of the pony's head and neck. If your back is too stiff, you will bump up and down in the saddle, which is very uncomfortable for both you and your pony.

The gallop This is a faster version of the canter but is ridden in a slightly different manner. The rider needs to get her weight further forward in order not to lose balance or get 'left behind'. This is done by shortening the reins so that the straight line from the elbow through the hand to the horse's mouth can be kept, leaning forward and taking the weight out of the saddle. If you shorten the stirrup-leathers slightly, it will help you to transfer your weight to your knees and stirrups.

The gallop. The rider's weight is now forward on the knees and stirrups.

All these things will be taught to you at a good riding school, and as your competence increases so will your confidence. Soon the time will come when you feel ready to cope with a pony of your own. But even then, it is sensible to continue to have a lesson from time to time. It is much too easy to slip into bad habits unknowingly. A good rider should never stop trying to improve.

CHAPTER 2

Choosing the right pony

You have completed your series of riding lessons. You have acquired the skills necessary to handle a pony both in a school and out on a ride. You have probably learned to remove a saddle and bridle and, if the riding school you went to was a good one, you no doubt know how to put a saddle and bridle *on*. No wonder you have been badgering your parents for the last six months to get you a pony of your own.

At last, the firm 'No' has passed through the 'Maybe' stage and reached a committed 'Yes'. So now you are looking for a pony.

It is important that you realize straightaway that you are still learning. There are many aspects of owning a pony which never arise while you are still at the riding school. The most important of these is responsibility. When an animal is dependent on you for its welfare, you have taken on a duty which can *never* be shirked. However much you might want to join your non-riding friends for an outing to the local swimming-pool or ice-rink, you cannot go until you have completed your duty to your pony.

Fortunately, most pony-owners undertake this responsibility both willingly and eagerly. You will be rewarded a hundred times over by the fun and companionship that a pony brings, but you may have to make some sacrifices. It is best to be aware of this at the outset.

Now for the pony itself. A first pony must be reliable, kind, generous and willing. It must give you confidence because there will be plenty of times when you have to cope with it on your own, with no comforting riding instructor around to help you. If your parents are totally ignorant of horses, you will be the only 'expert' in your household.

The choice of a first pony must therefore be made with extreme care.

FINDING A PONY

Ponies are bought and sold in four different ways: by word of mouth; through advertisements in riding and local papers; through a dealer; and at auction.

Word of mouth

This is clearly an excellent method of finding a suitable pony. Your best plan is to tell your friends that your parents have finally agreed to get you a pony. Ask if they know of anyone who is looking for a likely buyer. If you are lucky, the word will come back that someone is selling their child's first pony because she is now going on to something bigger, and they would be only too pleased to let you try it because it would save them the bother of having to advertise.

Advertisements in papers

This is the most usual market-place for horses and ponies and you only have to look at the small ads section of any of the riding magazines to realize that hundreds of ponies change hands every week. It has its risks though. A pony's good points will be emphasized in the advertisement, but it is up to the prospective buyer to discover its faults. Advertisements also have their own jargon. 'Bombproof' should mean that the pony is generally unflappable, even when it meets a combine harvester or a fleet of motor-cyclists. 'Quiet to catch, shoe, box, clip' means that it is reasonably easy to catch when it is loose in a field, that it is not afraid of the farrier, that it will go in and out of a trailer without fuss and that it doesn't mind having its coat clipped. 'A real confidence-giver' should mean just what it says.

'Not a novice ride' would be an unlikely candidate for a first pony. It could mean that it is a lively pony; on the other hand, it could be a polite way of saying that it 'bombs off' at the slightest provocation.

Through a dealer

This is often a good way of buying a pony, although it won't be the cheapest. The dealer has to earn his living, after all. A good dealer, with a reputation to keep up, will go to endless trouble to find the right pony for you and will often agree to take it back if it proves unsuitable. Sometimes a dealer may be able to offer you the choice of three or four ponies. It is important, however, that you know *exactly* what you want. Do not be tempted to exaggerate either your ability or your experience.

At an auction

This is the place to get a pony fairly cheaply, but it is fraught with hazards. For one thing, you will not get a chance to try out the pony, although you will be allowed to examine it. It may carry a warranty of soundness but the period of the warranty is likely to be short, possibly only twenty-four hours. If you are considering visiting an auction sale in your search for a pony, it is absolutely vital that you go with someone who has had many years' experience with ponies.

WHAT TO LOOK FOR

Temperament, age, size and conformation are the four most important considerations in choosing a pony.

Temperament

This means the way in which the pony behaves, and it can make all the difference between a pony which is absolutely right for you and one which would be better with somebody else. You, too, have a temperament and if yours and the pony's match then you have the perfect combination. So be honest with yourself. If you are nervous, admit it. If you really prefer to go slowly and stay at the back of the ride, look for a pony which shares your attitude. If you are a daydreamer, look for a sure-footed pony which will carry you safely however much your mind wanders. If, on the other hand, you like to lead the way and are always the first over a jump or into an adventure, you will need a bold, forward-going pony which is happy to take the lead.

The best way to find out if the pony you are trying out is the one for you is to ask. It is very difficult for anyone asked a direct question to answer with a barefaced lie. On the other hand, if you don't ask, the seller may easily forget to give you the information you most need, not necessarily because they want to deceive you but simply because it never occurred to them that you might want to know.

Age

Many people feel that a pony is not worth buying unless it is young, by which they mean five or six years old. Usually, they are thinking of the time when they will have to sell the pony themselves, when it will be two or three years older and perhaps harder to sell. It is a great pity that youth has assumed so much importance. The ideal age for a first pony is about fifteen years old or more. By that age, it has learned wisdom and experience and still has ten to fifteen years of honest service to come. The best first pony this author ever knew was still giving confidence to beginners, guiding them through their first gymkhanas and taking care of them on rides at the age of thirty-five.

Certainly, a first pony should be at least eight years old. No pony should be sold to an inexperienced home under the age of four. Between five and eight it may be suitable for a beginner, but the chances are that it is quiet and docile because it is young. Of course, very old ponies will require more looking after and as they grow even older and you grow more ambitious they will not be able to manage the work you want them to do. But by that time, you will no longer be a beginner and it will be time to let the pony go to another novice to start the confidence-giving process all over again.

Size

It is just as foolish to get a pony that is too big for you as to buy one that is too small. Remember that if you are having to look after the pony all by yourself, you must be able to saddle and bridle it and groom it properly without having to stand on a box. You must also be able to get on the pony without the aid of a mounting-block. And it helps if you can vault on bareback.

Most native ponies may be small, but they are strong and sturdy and perfectly capable of carrying an adult. As a rough guide to matching height of pony and age of child, the following table will help.

Pony's height	Age of child
Under 11 hh	Under 7
11 to 12 hh	7 to 9
12.1 to 13 hh	10 to 13
13.1 to 14.2 hh	12 to 17
14.2 to 15.2 hh	15 to 17

A hand (hh) measures 4 in (approximately 10cm) and the height of a pony is taken from the withers, the highest point of its shoulder, to the ground.

Your own build is also important, of course. If you are small for your age, you can keep a small pony for longer than your gangling friends. Your age becomes vital only when you are entering competitions.

Conformation

Conformation means the pony's build. The way a pony is made affects its movements, and faults in conformation can lead to problems in fitting a saddle. But just as you may feel that your nose is too big or your legs too fat and that you would never win a beauty contest, so a pony can have small faults which make it useless for a showing class but do not affect its performance elsewhere.

However, here are some points to bear in mind:

Round, broad-backed ponies can be uncomfortable to ride, especially if you are not very tall. If your legs are stretched wide, you will not be able to give the leg-aids properly and this will make it difficult for you to improve your riding and your pony's ability. You may also have difficulty finding a saddle which fits properly and does not slip.

Short-withered ponies can have trouble with their saddles. A *low wither* may cause the saddle to slip forward and you will need a crupper to keep it in place. *High-withered ponies* can suffer the opposite problem – the saddle slips back or makes the pony sore.

Narrow-chested, flat-ribbed ponies may lack stamina. If their forelegs are too close together, they may not be very sure-footed and therefore may be likely to stumble or even fall.

Thick-necked ponies can be very strong. They may also lean on the bit, which is uncomfortable and tiring for the rider.

Ponies with a low head carriage are also tiring to ride. However, a low head carriage may be due to lack of schooling rather than poor conformation and careful riding can overcome the problem. But for a beginner, it is best to choose a pony with a good head carriage. *A high head carriage* may make the pony difficult

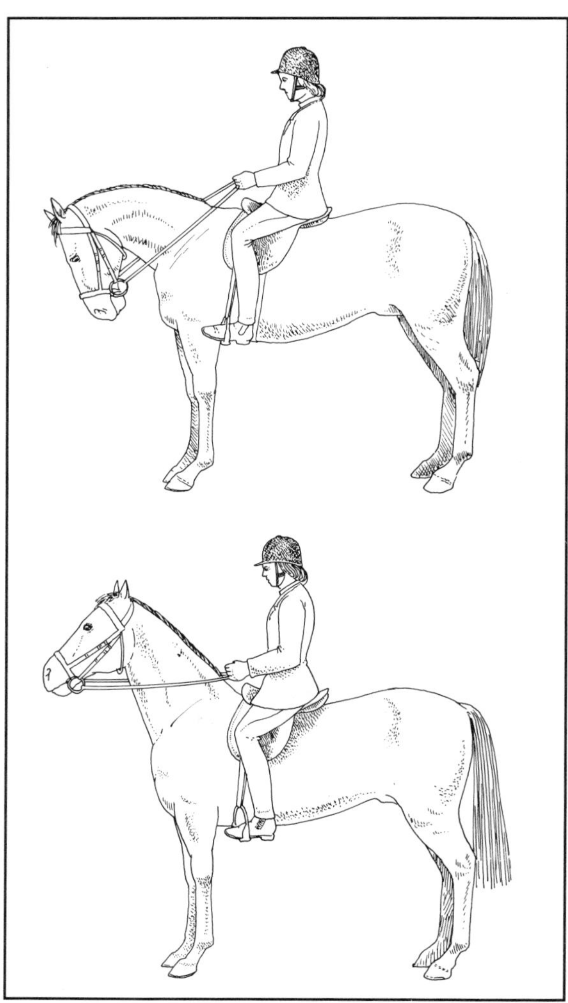

Two ponies to avoid. **Top** The pony is over-bent. By tucking his head in, he is able to evade the bit. Careful schooling, however, could correct this fault. **Bottom** This pony has a heavy head and a short, thick neck. No amount of schooling could correct this fault of conformation.

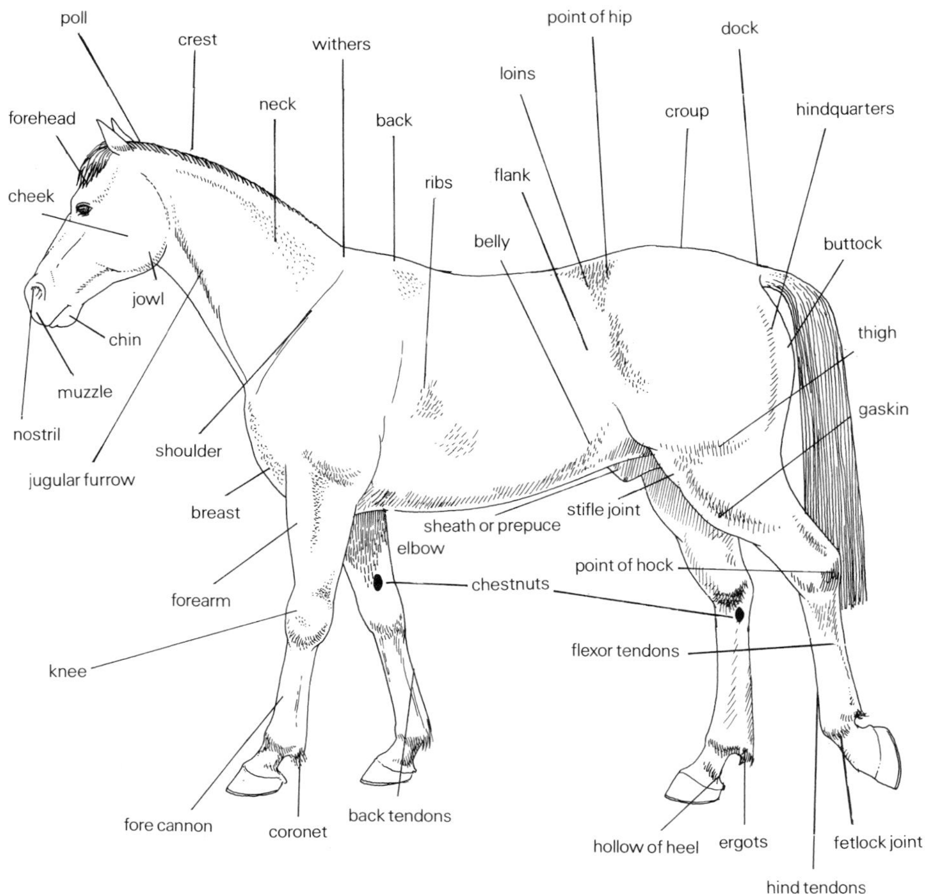

The points of the horse.

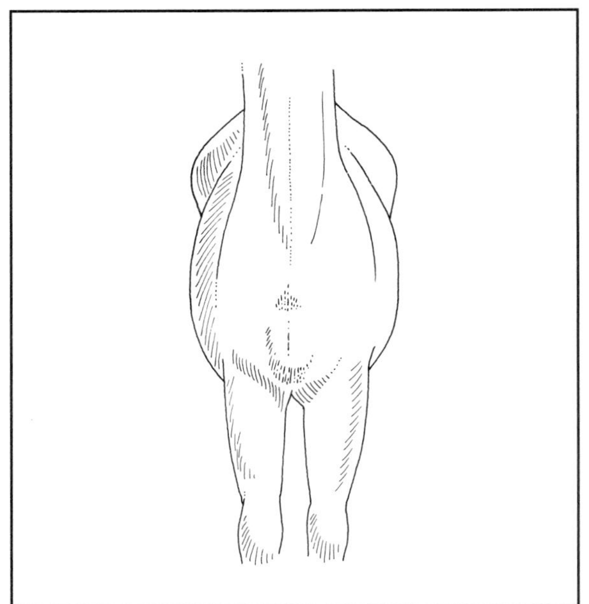

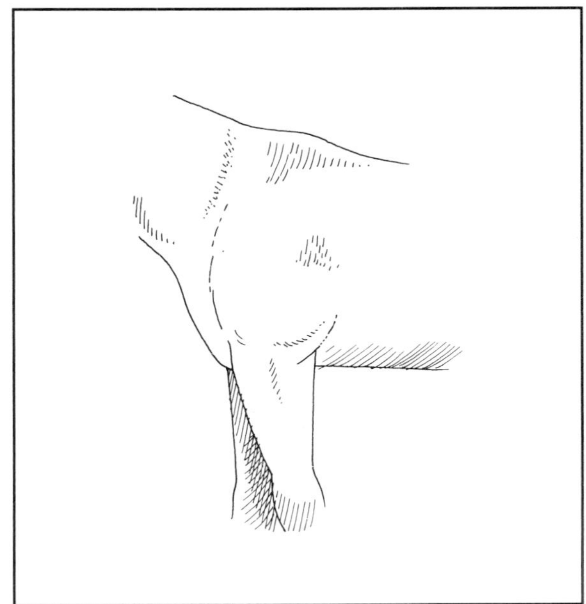

Left A narrow-breasted pony. **Right** A shallow-chested pony.

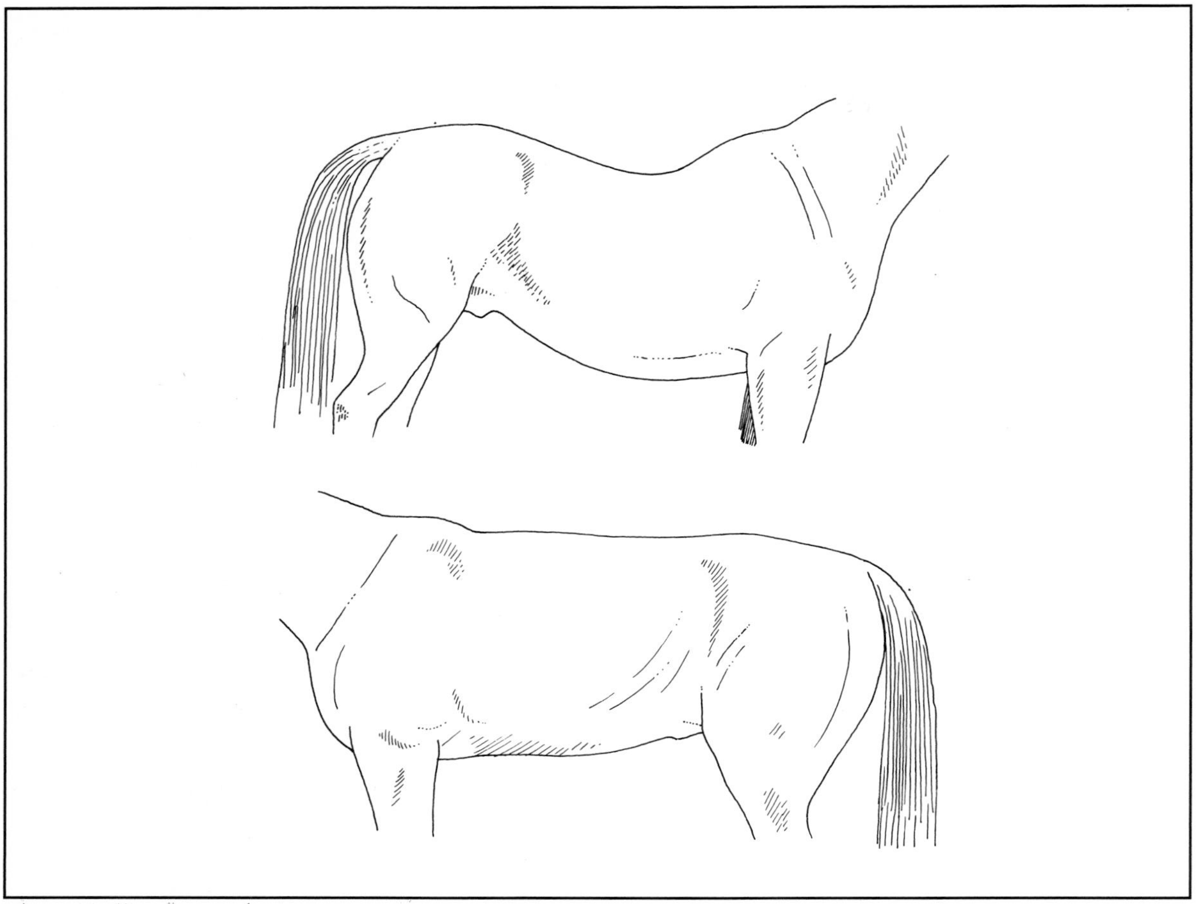

Two more faults to avoid. **Top** A Hollow-back. **Above** A Roach back.

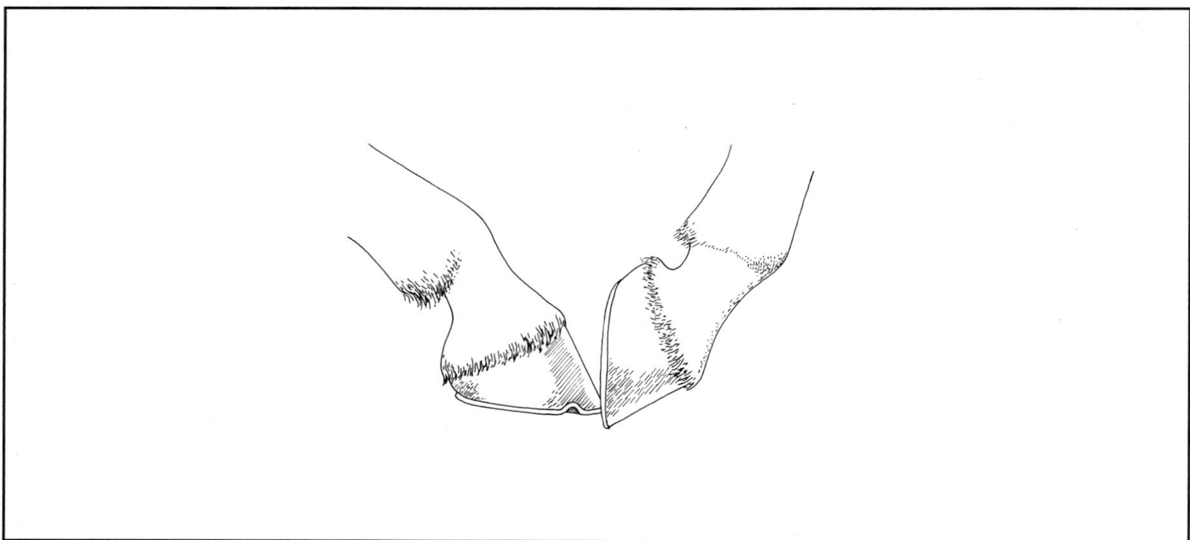

Forging. This happens when the toe of the hind shoe strikes the underneath of the front shoe, making a noticeable clicking noise. It is caused by a weakness in conformation, and the only remedy lies in the shoeing. The blacksmith should be consulted.

to control, particularly if it sticks its nose in the air. Again, it is wise to avoid such a pony if you have very little experience.

Long-backed ponies or those with high-stepping action are uncomfortable riding ponies.

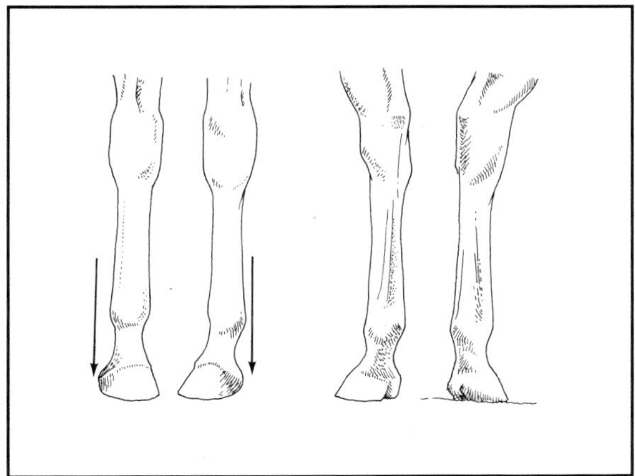

Left Knock-kneed and pigeon-toed. **Right** Cow-hocked.

Cow-hocked or knock-kneed ponies may have an awkward action and there is a danger of the legs interfering with one another. Unless the pony is supremely suitable for you in every other way, you should let your search for the right pony continue.

Of course there is one other factor in all this which will have an effect on the pony you eventually end up with, and that is cost. Study the advertisements to get some idea of the current prices expected for a pony of the type you require. It is only when the pony has had considerable success in competitions that its price is much higher than the average.

GOING TO LOOK AT A PONY

It is probably useless to say to anyone who is going to look at a pony that it is wise not to make up your mind too quickly. Whatever made you decide to go in the first place – the wording of the advertisement, a telephone call from a friend or the horse dealer – you already will have mentally given the pony qualities which have never been claimed by the person who is selling it. You will be 90 per cent certain that this is just the pony for you.

Nothing anyone can say will stop this secret feeling, but do beware of it. It will encourage you to overlook faults and make excuses if the pony does not come up to scratch: 'It doesn't know me. It'll be different when I get it home.' The truth is, of course, that this is unlikely, so be sensible. Take an experienced person with you who can look at the pony with an objective eye.

When you have arranged to visit the pony, try to be there on time; if you cannot make it, telephone the owners to let them know. There is nothing more frustrating for the seller than, after preparing a pony for inspection, she has to hang about for hours waiting for the purchasers to turn up.

It is natural for the seller to want to present the pony in the best possible light, so you will doubtless find it well groomed, with oiled hooves and clean tack. It is rare for the sellers to wait until you arrive before collecting the pony from the field and giving it a quick rub over, before allowing you to try it, although this would give you a very good idea of the pony's virtues. It is helpful, for example, to see how good the pony is about being caught. Otherwise you will just have to ask.

You should take along a list of questions that you have prepared in advance, to put to the sellers when you have tried out the pony. Such a list could include:

Is it easy to catch?

Will it stay in a field by itself?

Is it good-tempered and quiet to handle, especially when eating food?

Is it good-tempered with other ponies?

Will it go well on its own, or does it become nappy when asked to leave a group of ponies? Animals which have been used in riding schools, for example, often become impossibly difficult when they are by themselves.

Will it go into a trailer without fuss?

Is it good in traffic?

Does it behave well with the blacksmith or vet?

Is it head-shy? Some ponies, which have been ill-treated in their youth, object to having their ears touched. This could make things difficult for you when you have to bridle the pony yourself.

You should, if you can, ride the pony before deciding whether to buy him or not. The sellers may suggest that their child or friend puts the pony through its paces first and this will give you a good idea of how the pony goes for someone he knows. But you should also ride him, even though you may make allowances for you and the pony being strangers to each other. You may, for example, find difficulty in getting him to canter, mainly because you are rather inexperienced and the pony knows it. Also try leading him in-hand, and check yourself that the pony doesn't mind having his feet picked up in turn.

On the pony's general suitability and soundness, you should listen to the advice given you by a knowledgeable friend, whose experienced eye may detect faults which are not apparent to you.

While it is a good idea to have the pony checked by a vet before you buy it, it is perfectly possible to spot a healthy pony when you see one.

A healthy pony is alert, bright-eyed and has a shine to its coat. Check that its feet are in good condition. If the hooves are cracked or overlong, it suggests that the present owners have not been taking care of them properly. A heavily ridged hoof is an indication that the pony has at some time in the recent past suffered from *laminitis* (see page 83). An inexperienced owner should avoid a pony which has had laminitis.

Another disease to which some ponies are prone is *sweet itch* (see page 84). This is a skin condition caused by an allergy to biting insects and is apparent only in the summer months. Sweet itch does not occur in the winter months and if you are buying a pony in the early spring there may be no signs of the problem. Always ask about sweet itch. You should not buy a pony which suffers from it unless you have your own stable and field next to your house.

Once you have found the pony which is perfect for you, the time has come to bring it home.

CHAPTER 3

Keeping a pony in a field

A first pony does *not* need a stable. Contrary to what anyone may tell you, a pony's natural habitat is out-of-doors, summer and winter alike. At this stage in your pony-ownership, a stable is an unnecessary luxury.

It does, however, need a secure field with reasonable grazing, a regular supply of fresh water, and some sort of wind-break.

THE RIGHT FIELD

It is not possible to be definite about the amount of grazing a pony requires. Much depends on the size of the pony and the quality and nutritional value of the grass available. As a general rule, however, a single pony needs one to two acres to keep it healthy throughout the year. Supplementary feeding will be necessary in the winter.

Many pony-owners do not have their own field and lucky indeed is the child with access to unlimited grazing. Most children, through their parents, have to rent grazing and this can be an expensive item in the maintenance costs of one pony.

A field next to your house, particularly one which is owned by your family, is the ideal situation. The nearest grazing, available to rent, may be some distance away and this can present problems when feeding in the winter or when you want to ride.

Some farmers are willing to let out a field on a grass-rent basis. This means that you pay rent for the grazing rights, usually on a renewable lease for a period of one year less one day, with the rent payable quarterly, and no limit to the number of animals you wish to graze on the field at any one time.

Other farmers and land-owners will rent out grazing on the basis of a weekly payment per pony. This is a very common arrangement, which can be terminated by an agreed period of notice on either side, normally four weeks or one month. The land-owner is financially responsible for the upkeep of the fencing and the provision of water, but it is your responsibility to see that any repairs are carried out.

The ideal field is about two to three acres in size, with undulating ground, secure post-and-rail fencing, a high hedge to act as a wind-break, and a gravel-bottomed stream, or spring-fed pond, to provide fresh water.

Not many fields reach this ideal, however. Some may be so big that it takes you half an hour to *find* your pony, let alone catch him. Another may be less than an acre in size and must be rested from time to time to help preserve the grazing. Water is often mains-supplied, either piped in to an automatic trough or controlled by a tap, from which you will need a hose-pipe to fill a makeshift trough or buckets. If the field lacks any form of wind-break, even a natural hollow in the ground, you will have to supply a field shelter. And the fencing is likely to be barbed wire.

None of this matters too much as long as what you have, you look after properly.

Grazing

Many farmers do not like having horses on their land because of their wasteful grazing habits. Horses look for the tastiest grasses, trampling down other nutritious grasses in the process. Where they have left their droppings, the grass grows coarse and rank, allowing weeds, such as docks, nettles and thistles, to develop. In time, a field which is exclusively and permanently grazed by horses grows patchy in appearance. The ground becomes almost bare in some places and thickly and coarsely grassed in others. If the field is not properly looked after, it will become horse-sick and infested with worm parasites, which in turn infect the ponies grazing on it.

Fortunately, there are various ways in which a small area of grazing can be kept in reasonably good condition. The first is to pick up the droppings regularly and remove them to a muck-heap. This needs to be a daily chore, for even only a couple of ponies can produce a large amount of manure in a very short time.

The second is to rest the field for periods of six weeks to three months. During this time, the field should be topped with a mower, which cuts down the coarse grass and allows the better grasses to grow. Harrowing will also help. It spreads the droppings around (if you haven't had time to pick them up) so that they dry out, and the parasites then die.

Grazing other livestock, such as bullocks or sheep, in the field is extremely beneficial. They eat off the coarse grass and destroy the horse parasites, which cannot harm the sheep or bullocks.

Proper land-care means that you can keep a pony healthy on a smaller area of grazing than would otherwise be the case. Two ponies, for example, can live easily in two one-acre paddocks, as long as each paddock is given time to rest and recover.

Fencing

The most secure form of fencing is post-and-rail, either standing alone or combined with a hedge. It is expensive to buy and erect but it lasts a long time. The cheapest fencing is wire, either plain or barbed. To be secure, at least three strands of plain wire will be needed (four or five are better), properly stretched and fastened to posts set firmly in the ground. The bottom strand should be at least 30cm (12 in) from the ground. Barbed wire is not advisable because it is dangerous if it is not really taut, but for those who have to rent someone else's field there may be no other choice. You must be extra vigilant with

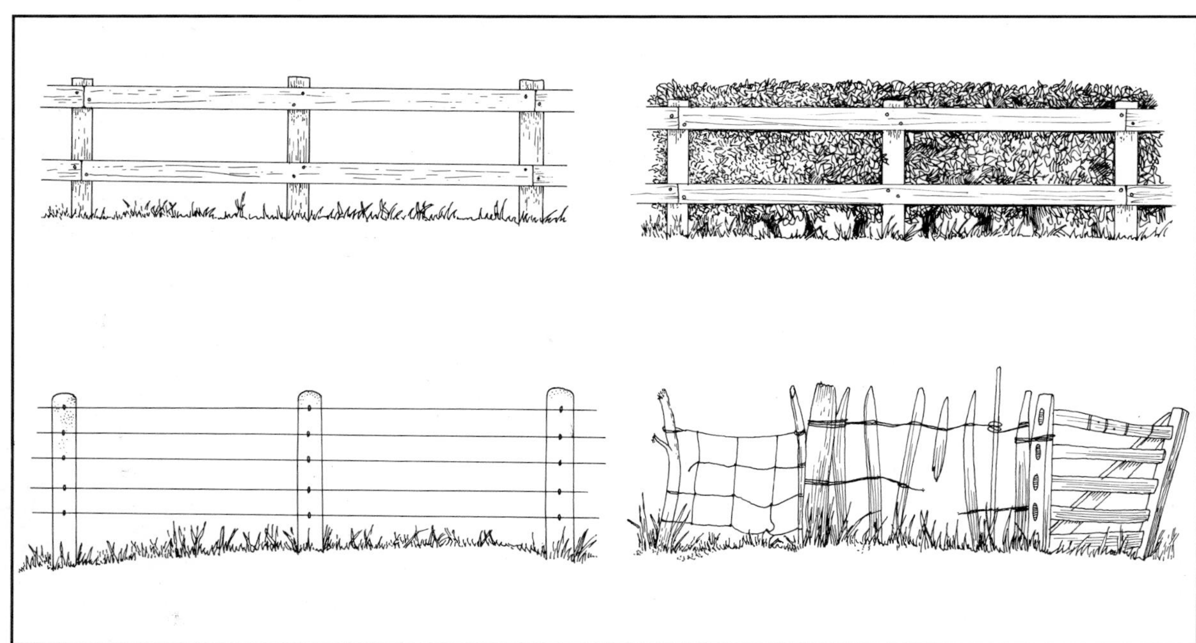

Top left Plain post-and-rail.
Top right Post-and-rail fence, with hedge behind.
Bottom left Plain wire fence, properly erected.

Bottom right Bad fencing. Sheep netting is dangerous as the pony may get his hoof caught in it; chestnut paling may be used if it is protected by a hedge but not alone, as here; the railed gate is too flimsy.

a wire fence of any kind as the wire may become slack and the posts may loosen.

If there is a hedge round the field, it may need strengthening with an inner post-and-rail fence. It is a good idea to allow the hedge to grow high along the side from which the prevailing wind blows as this will provide the necessary wind-break. Always check that there is no yew in the hedge because yew is extremely poisonous.

Gate

A proper field gate is best as long as it swings clear of the ground and the gatepost is firm. The access to the field should be wide enough to allow a tractor through when the field needs cutting, although a narrower gate, such as a hunting gate, would be quite wide enough for ponies. The gate-fastening should be pony-proof, and there are plenty of patent latches and fastenings on the market. Gates, however, do tend to drop in time, making the fastenings difficult to manage. If this happens and the gate cannot be rehung, the safest form of fastening is a chain with a clip or ring through which the other end passes. Baler twine, which goes right round the gatepost and through the gate to be tied in a double bow, is a cheap alternative but not very pretty.

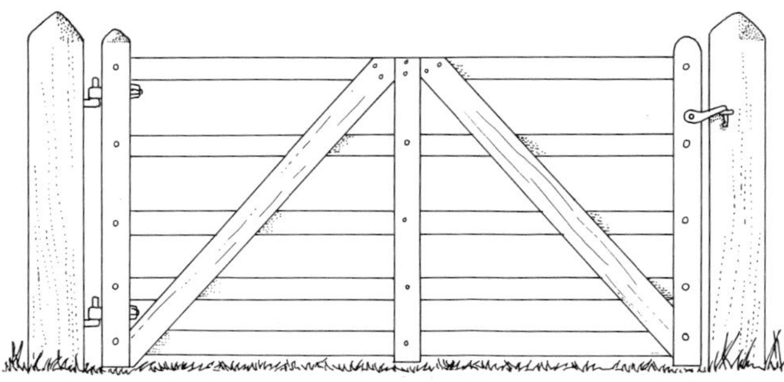

A five-barred gate, well hung.

Water

In the absence of a stream or spring-fed pond, some form of trough must be provided. A stagnant pond, or a stream with high banks or thick mud at the bottom should be fenced off. Automatic troughs are found on most farms that have piped mains water. They are fed by an underground pipe and controlled by a ball-valve which keeps the water at a certain level. Sometimes a tap is used to control the flow of water and, for safety's sake, the pipe leading to the tap should hug the side of the trough. If the nearest water tap is some way away, you will have to buy a hose-pipe to transfer water to the trough.

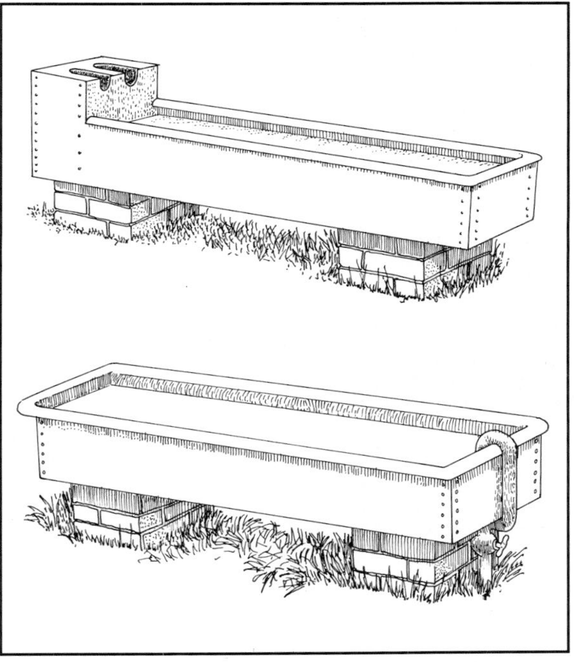

Top Automatic water trough. **Above** Water trough with supply pipe hugging the end of the trough.

From time to time, the trough should be emptied and scrubbed out to remove any algae and scum which has formed. Remember that in winter, the trough may freeze over or the water supply may freeze. In that case, you will have to carry buckets to the field from the nearest house. A rubber ball left floating on the surface of the water helps to keep it free from light ice.

Shelter

Most ponies and horses are unconcerned by rain and snow. They dislike wind, however, and like to stand in the lee of a wall, hedge or building, or even in a hollow in the ground, when a gale is blowing. In summer, they need protection from the hot sun and flies and will chose to stand in the shadow of a tree. If there is no suitable tree available, a field shelter is the answer. This is a three-sided shed positioned so that the opening faces away from the prevailing wind. It

An open-sided field shelter provides protection for both winter and summer.

should be big enough to prevent one pony from being cornered by others in the field. If your field has such a shelter, you will almost certainly find that your pony goes inside it more often in the summer-time.

COMPANIONSHIP

Although many ponies can and will live alone, they are better off in company. They are herd animals by nature and need friends of their own kind. When you get your new pony, you should try to provide him with a companion. Many people share a field with a friend, and this works very well as long as the owner of the other pony is indeed your friend. Your two families can share the responsibilities and costs of feeding, watering and inspecting the ponies, and of maintaining the fencing and the quality of the pasture. There will always be someone nearby who knows your pony and can look after it while you are away on holiday or if you are ill. Best of all, you have someone with whom to ride and to share the joys of owning a pony.

CHECKING THE FIELD

Before turning a pony out into a field, always make a careful check for safety. Look at the fencing and repair any damage.

See that none of the following poisonous plants are within reach. All parts of the *yew* are dangerous. It is highly poisonous and usually fatal. *Deadly nightshade*, which grows in hedgerows, is also dangerous. *Ragwort*, a tall, yellow-flowered plant, is poisonous when dead. If ragwort is growing in your field, you will spot it during the summer months. Pull it up while it is in full flower and remove it to a bonfire. *Never* leave pulled ragwort lying around on the ground. *Acorns* are harmful if eaten to excess. *Bracken* has long-term ill-effects if it is eaten over lengthy periods of time. Garden shrubs such as *privet* or *laurel* are poisonous, but the dead leaves

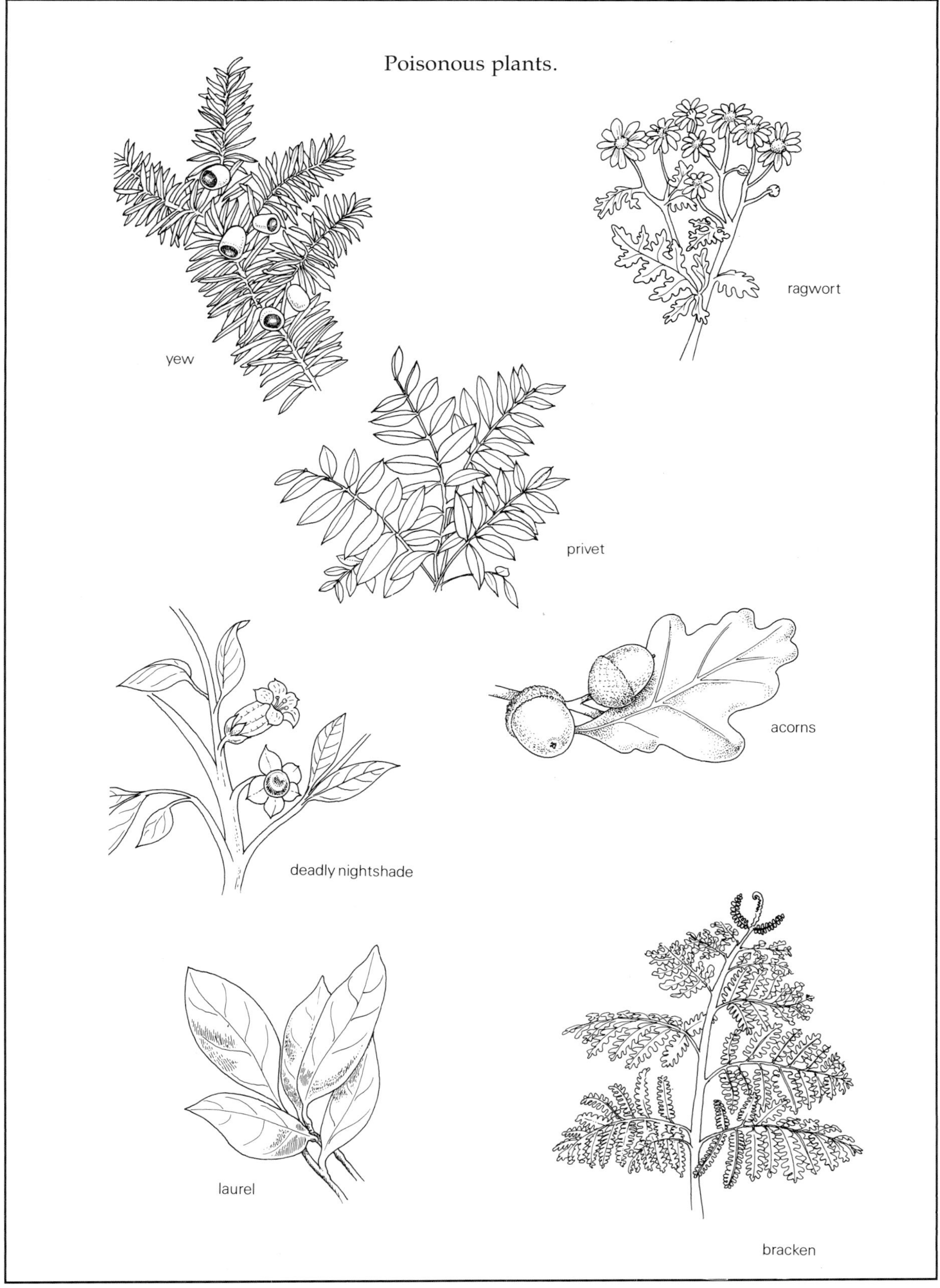

Poisonous plants.

are more dangerous than the living plants.

If your field is bordered by gardens, do make certain that the householders are not throwing clippings into the field, and warn the neighbours that they should not give lawn mowings to ponies. Their actions, however kindly meant, could make your pony very ill, as lawn mowings ferment quickly.

Finally, especially if a public footpath runs by the field, check that plastic bags, cans and bottles have not found their way over the fence. Cans and broken bottles can cause nasty injuries and a plastic bag is dangerous if the pony eats it by mistake.

TURNING OUT A PONY

The moment when you bring your new pony home for the first time is an exciting one, but do remember that it is bewildering for him. It is rather like starting at a new school, but whereas you have the chance to prepare yourself mentally for the ordeal, the pony has no idea what is happening to him. He started the day in familiar surroundings and now he has been taken to a completely strange place, probably in a trailer or horse-box from which he cannot see out. He may well be used to travelling but, before, he always emerged to the excited sounds of a show or rally.

Give him time to look around and settle down. However much you may be longing to ride him and to show him off to your friends, wait a day or two.

The best time for him to arrive is in the morning, so that he will have many hours of daylight left to explore his new home. This is particularly important if he is to join other ponies in the field. The old hands are sure to crowd round him, anxious to inspect the newcomer, and there will no doubt be some squealing and mild kicking. Normally, the 'getting to know you' routine takes about half an hour. After that, the new pony will begin to graze a little apart from the others. Later on, his place in the pecking order will be established and he will become a recognized member of the herd. He may eventually end up the boss of the field – the smallest ponies are often the bossiest – eating the best hay, having the first drink at the water trough, finishing up the other ponies' food.

It is sensible to leave his headcollar on him while he is turned out in the field, however easy to catch he may be. He has no idea who you are, after all, and may well be reluctant to come to you in the beginning. So be prepared to spend the first few days giving him titbits, catching him, making a fuss of him and letting him go again. You want him to look forward to seeing you. You and your pony are going to be friends and companions, hopefully for a long while, and the relationship should begin on a high note.

Quietly grazing. If a pony is at all difficult to catch, he can always be turned out in a headcollar.

CHAPTER 4
Essential equipment

The longer you have a pony of your own, the more equipment you will acquire. Luckily, a great many items are not necessary immediately, and your family and friends will soon find that choosing birthday and Christmas presents for you will become an easy task.

Some things, of course, are essential from the beginning. The pony – even a first pony – cannot do without: bridle; saddle; headcollar and lead-rope; tack cleaning kit; saddle and bridle racks; grooming kit; buckets.

Let us look at each item in turn.

Plain snaffle bridle, with cavesson noseband.

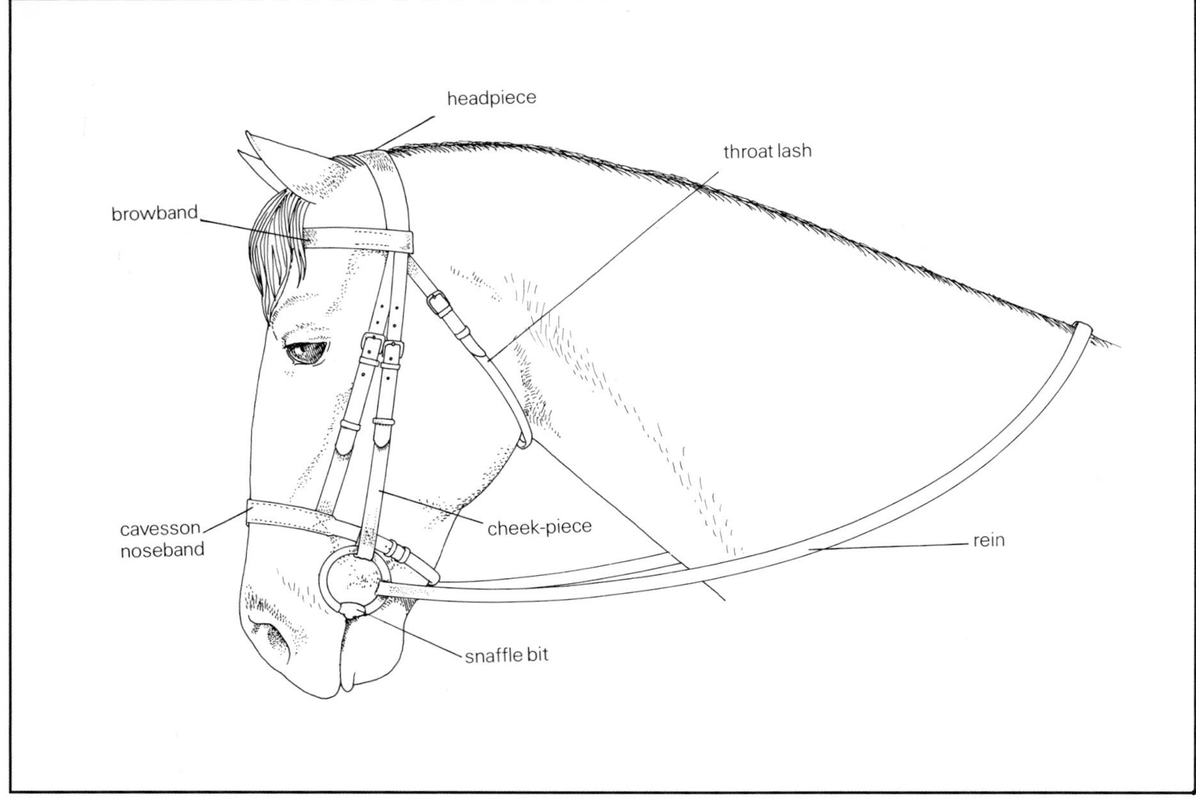

BRIDLE

A simple snaffle bridle should be adequate for your first pony. Bridles are sold in three sizes: pony, cob and full. However, ponies' heads vary in size. If your pony has a large head, and you are buying a new bridle for him, he may need the cob size. If possible, it is best to buy the pony's own bridle when you buy the pony. Even if it is old, it will serve him very well as long as it has been properly looked after.

Most bridles are made of leather. They can be adjusted easily to ensure a good fit, and can be taken apart for cleaning. It is important that you know the different parts of the bridle and how to put it together.

The *headpiece* is a leather strap which passes over the top of the pony's head behind his ears (the poll). It is made in one piece with the throat lash (or latch), which is a longer, thinner strap that comes under the pony's jaw-bone, buckles on the near side and prevents the bridle from coming off.

The *cheekpieces* are buckled to the headpiece and hang down on either side of the pony's face to support the bit. By raising or lowering the cheekpiece, the position of the bit in the mouth may be altered.

The *browband* is a strap with a loop at each end through which the headpiece passes. It runs across the pony's forehead and stops the headpiece from slipping back.

The *rein* is fixed to the bit rings and is usually in two parts, linked by a buckle.

The *bit* on a first pony should be a snaffle, usually jointed in the middle. It should be positioned so that it just wrinkles the corners of the pony's mouth. If it is too low it will

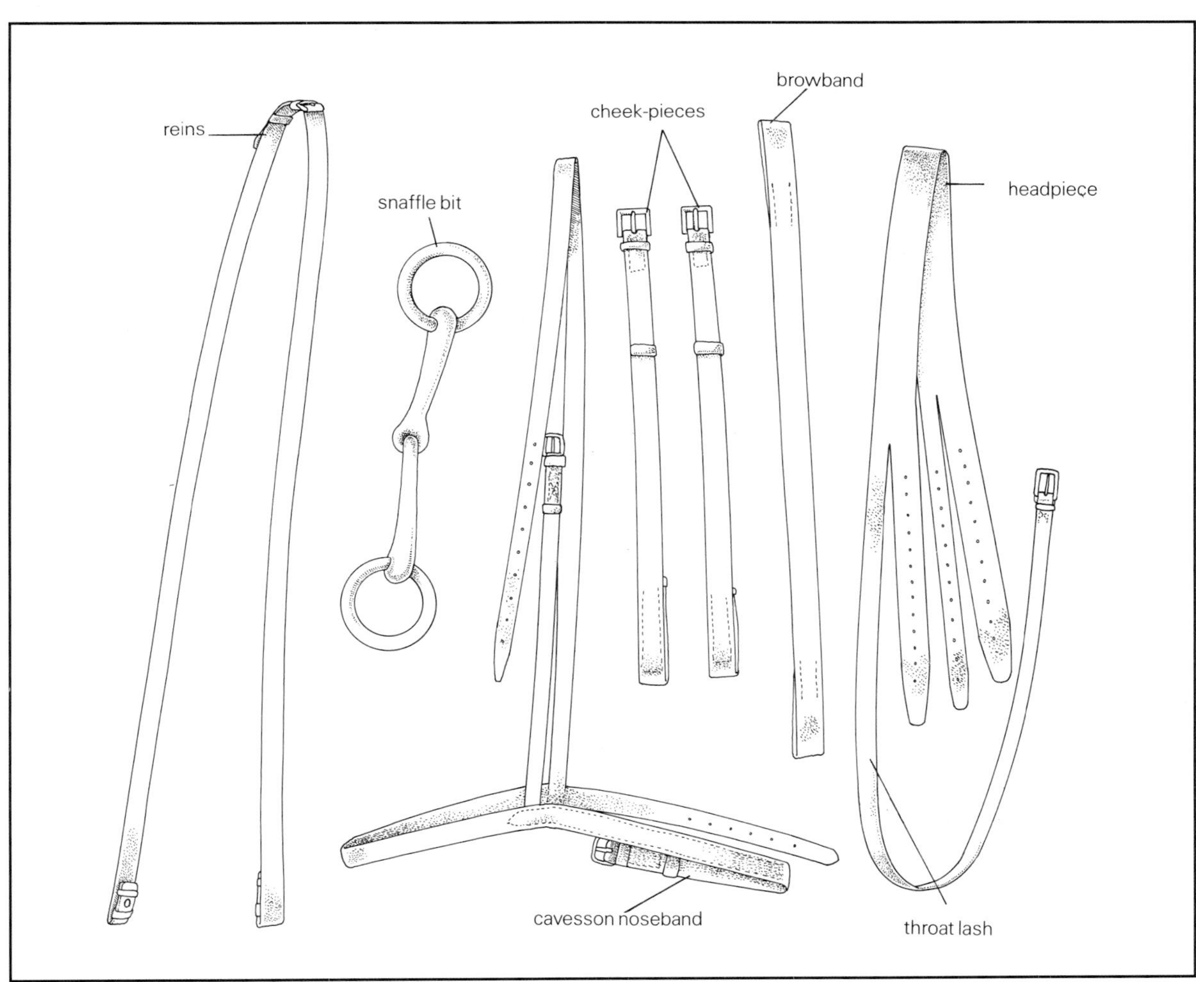

The parts of the snaffle bridle.

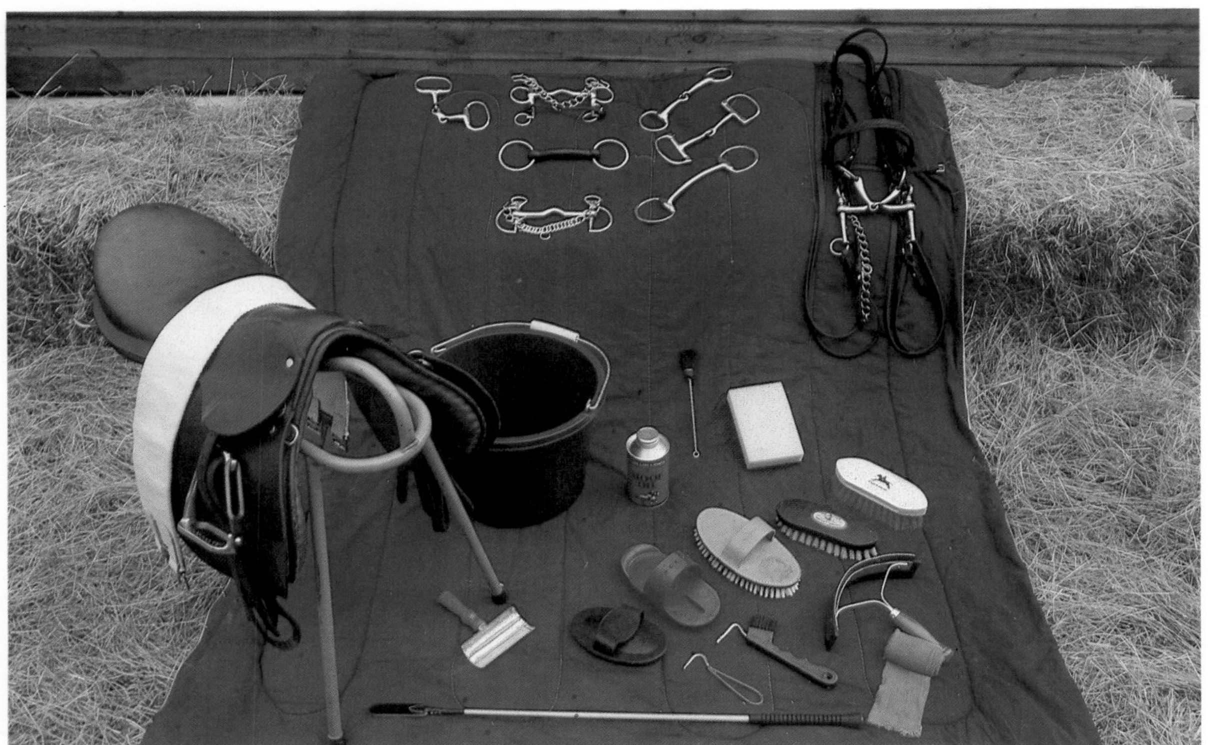

Above Equipment for the pony. **from left** Bits: French bridoon, Pelham, eggbutt snaffle, rubber snaffle D-cheeked snaffle, Kimblewick, straight-bar snaffle. Double bridle. General-purpose saddle, fitted with safety stirrups. Bracket. Grooming kit: hoof oil, hoof-oil brush, sponge, metal curry-comb, rubber curry-comb, plastic curry-comb, body brush, water brush, dandy brush, two hoof picks, sweat scraper, tail bandage. Whip.

Opposite A first pony should need no more than a plain snaffle bridle, with a cavesson noseband.

bang against the pony's teeth. It controls the pony in two ways. When pressure is put on the reins, it acts on the corner of the mouth and exerts a slight pull on the horse's poll or top of the head. The joint in the middle has a nut cracker action on the tongue. The tongue should lie under the mouthpiece of the bit.

The *noseband*, or *cavesson*, is held in place by a strap which goes over the pony's head, through the loops of the browband, and buckles on the near side. The strap lies under the headpiece. The diameter of the noseband can be adjusted by means of a buckle at the back. A cavesson serves no purpose unless the pony is being ridden in a standing martingale (and no first pony should need such a martingale). In this case the front end of the martingale is looped on to the noseband. The noseband, however, is regarded as important in making the pony look properly dressed.

In Western bridles, nosebands are not used, but then the whole Western style of riding is totally different from the English or Continental style practised in Europe and on the eastern side of America, and so are the saddles and bridles used. It may be tempting to remove your pony's noseband to give him a more real Western look. However, nosebands on their own have a habit of disappearing, and this can lead to disaster at showing time. The easiest way of keeping your bridle intact is never to separate the noseband from the rest of the bridle except when you are cleaning it.

SADDLE

The best saddle for general use is known as a general-purpose saddle. Here again, it is wise to buy the pony's own saddle at the time you buy the pony. However, it is very important for your own comfort and safety that the saddle should fit you as well as the pony. A good saddle carries the rider in the correct riding position without any discomfort to the horse and without forcing the rider's legs forwards or backwards.

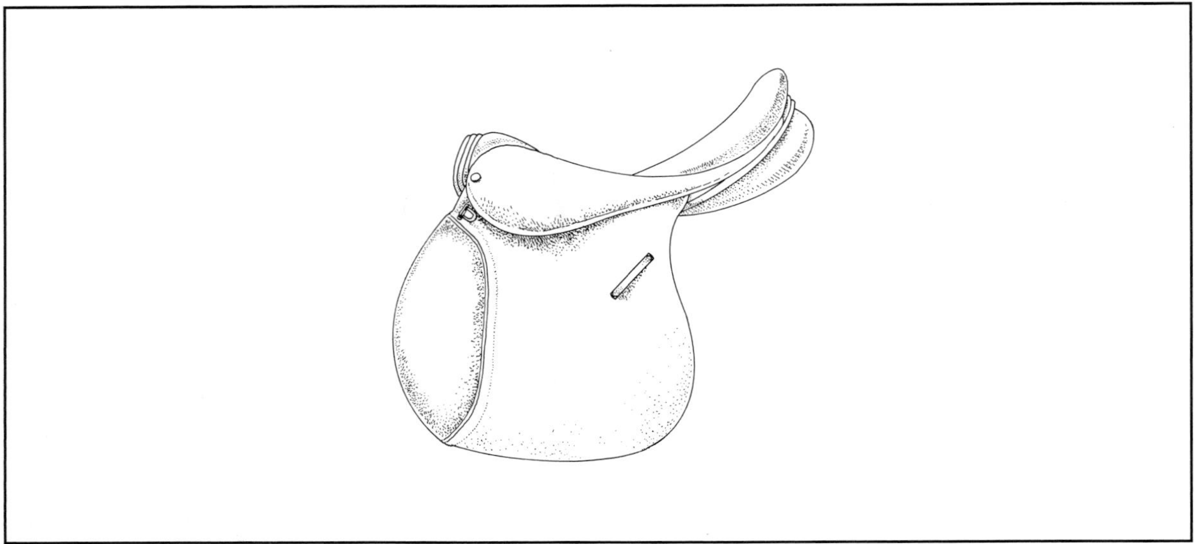

General-purpose saddle with knee roll.

A saddle is made up of several parts.

The *tree*, the skeleton of the saddle, determines the shape of the final product, and is therefore most important. It is traditionally made of laminated beechwood, although modern man-made materials, such as plastic and glass fibre, are used nowadays. A *spring-tree* has a piece of flexible steel set into it at the waist. Bands of *webbing* are stretched on to the framework to carry the stuffing and leather finish.

The *stuffing* may be of wool, felt or foam rubber, and the underside of the saddle should be sufficiently stuffed to create a gullet

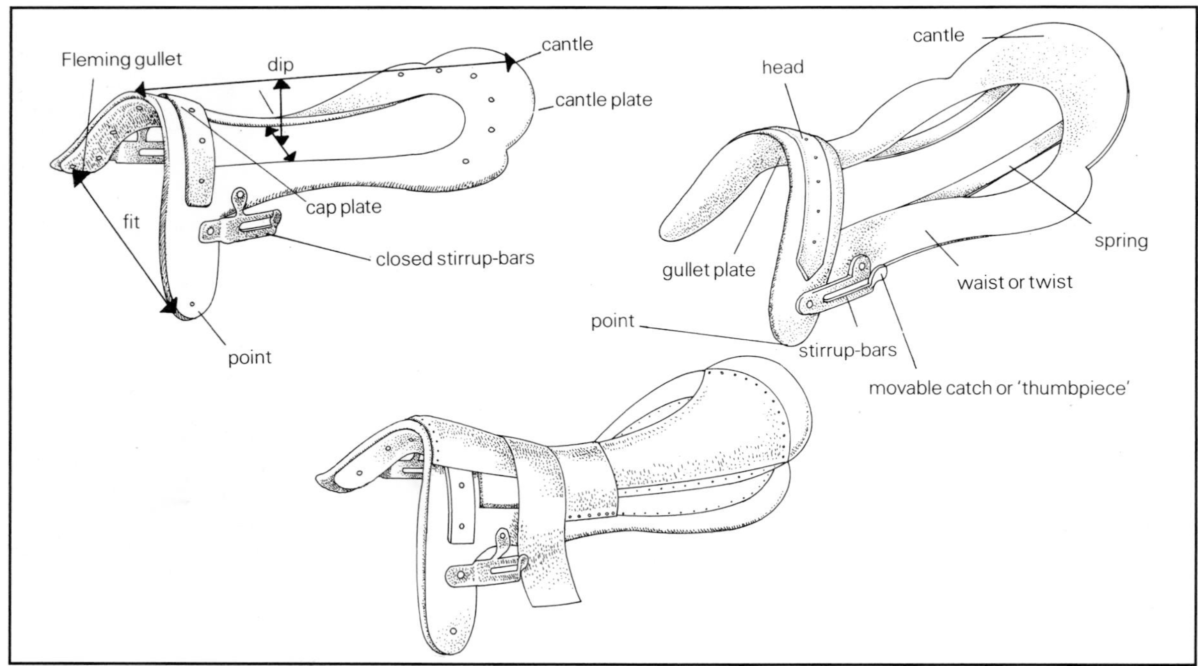

Saddle trees. **Top left** Ordinary tree. **Top right** Spring-tree. **Bottom** Spring-tree after straining.

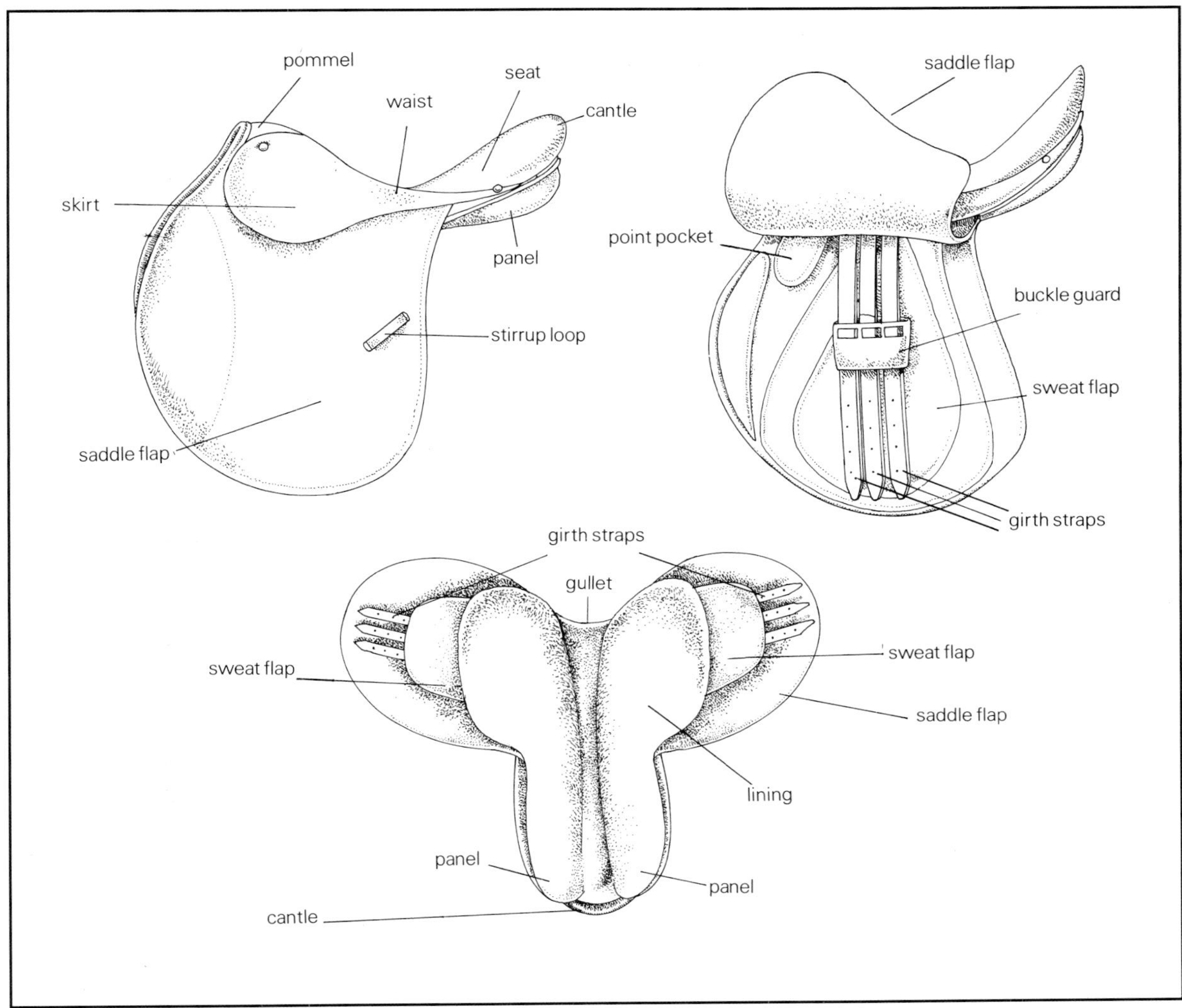

The parts of a saddle.

from the front to the back of the saddle and to give clearance over the pony's spine. Enough stuffing should be used on the seat to make the saddle comfortable for the rider.

Linings and leather panels and coverings are used to give the saddle its final familiar appearance.

There are three kinds of lining: linen, which is easy to clean, quick to dry and reasonably hard-wearing; serge, which is very absorbent, but wears quite quickly and is hard to clean; and leather, which cleans easily and lasts well, provided it is properly looked after.

The *panels* are the parts of the saddle closest to the horse. They carry the stuffing and lining. On a general-purpose saddle, the panels may have a roll of stuffing along each forward edge. These are known as knee-rolls, and are designed to give support to the rider's knees. There are two types: full panel and half panel. The first reaches to the bottom of the saddle flap, the second only half-way down. The *girth straps* rest on the panel, although in some saddles there is an additional piece of leather, called a *sweat flap*, which lies between the panel and the girth straps. Most saddles are fitted with three girth straps, although the girth has only two buckles. You should alternate the straps you use in order to keep the wear on the saddle even.

The outer panel of the saddle is called the *saddle flap* and it should hang down far enough to hide the ends of the girth straps. The small flap of leather which conceals the stirrup-bars is known as the *skirt*.

The metal *stirrup-bars* are attached to the tree. They are usually fitted with safety-catches, small hinged ends which can be raised or lowered. You should always ride with the catches in the down position, so that the stirrup-leathers will come off if you happen to fall and your foot is trapped in the stirrup. The catches are put up *only* when you are carrying the saddle.

Always use a pair of *buckle guards* when riding to protect the saddle flaps and panels from being damaged by the girth buckles.

Fitting a saddle

If you are buying a new saddle for your pony, the wisest plan is to try it on the pony in the presence of a qualified saddler, who will be able to advise you on whether any small adjustments can be made by altering the stuffing, or whether you should try a different saddle altogether. However, if you don't have an expert to advise you, remember the following points.

The saddle is designed to distribute the rider's weight over the muscular parts of the horse's back. A saddle which is too long may throw the rider's weight back on to the loins. If it is too forward cut, there may be too much weight on the front of the saddle, which could eventually lead to soreness; and it may impede the pony's movements.

There should be no weight on the spine; daylight should be visible from front to back along the gullet when you are mounted. Check also that the gullet is wide enough to prevent any pressure along the edges of the spine.

The front arch of the saddle must be high enough and wide enough to prevent any pinching of the horse's withers. Some horses have high withers and need a saddle with a high, narrow arch. The waist of the saddle should be fairly narrow and the seat should be deep. This will help to bring the rider into the correct position.

Check the stirrup-bars; when you are mounted they should be horizontal and parallel to the ground. The stirrup-leathers, which are attached to the bars, will then hang perpendicular to the ground and your legs will be in the right place.

A pony's conformation may create problems when it comes to fitting a saddle. On a pony with a high wither the saddle may slip back, and a breastplate could be needed to keep it in place. On a small pony, with a low,

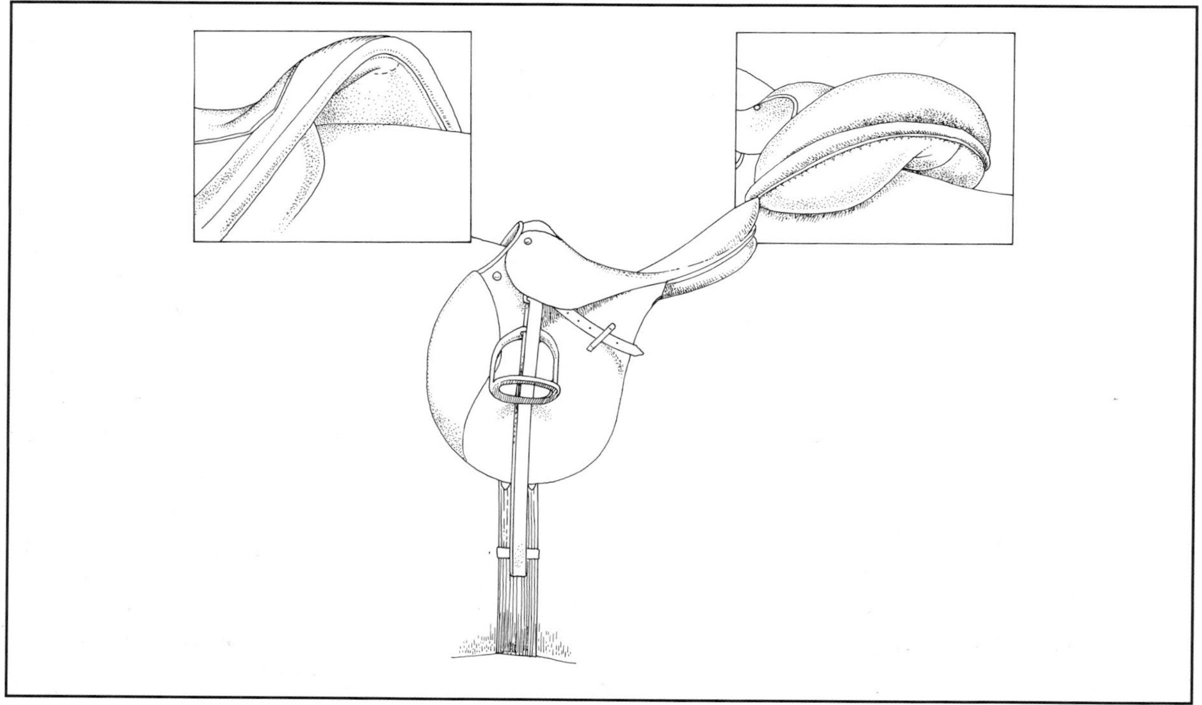

The saddle should fit properly, with adequate clearance over the spine. **Top Left** There should be no pressure on the withers by the front arch. **Top right** Daylight should be visible through the channel along the pony's spine.

flat wither, the saddle can slip forwards, and you would need a crupper to prevent this from happening.

Girths

Girths may be made of nylon, webbing, leather or lampwick.

Nylon girths are usually of single strands, linked at intervals by woven string and fitted with two buckles at each end. They are good general-purpose girths which grip well, especially on an unclipped pony. They can be washed easily and dry quickly.

Webbing girths are made of a single straight piece of webbing with one buckle at either end. They are inexpensive but can break. Two webbing girths should always be used together, one overlapping the other. Unless they are well looked after, they can get stiff with sweat and cause chafing.

Leather girths are hard-wearing but must be cared for properly if they are to stay soft and supple. There are three popular types. The Balding is divided into three along the centre portion. These three strips are then crossed over one another and stitched in place. The effect is to make the girth narrower at the places where it passes behind the horse's forelegs. The Atherstone is cut to a shape similar to the Balding, but it is one piece. To reinforce it, a strip of leather is sewn along its length. The Three-fold consists of a wide piece of leather folded into three. All these girths are fitted with two buckles at each end. The stitching on leather girths should always be carefully checked.

The *Lampwick* is a very soft girth of tubular, stocking-like material which stretches during use but goes back into shape afterwards. It has an inner lining of leather or webbing. It is fitted with two buckles at either end.

The *Cottage Craft* girth has become extremely popular in recent years. It is a straight girth of padded nylon material, reinforced with nylon webbing. Its advantages are that it can be easily washed and dried, and it does not chafe. It comes in a variety of colours and each end has two buckles.

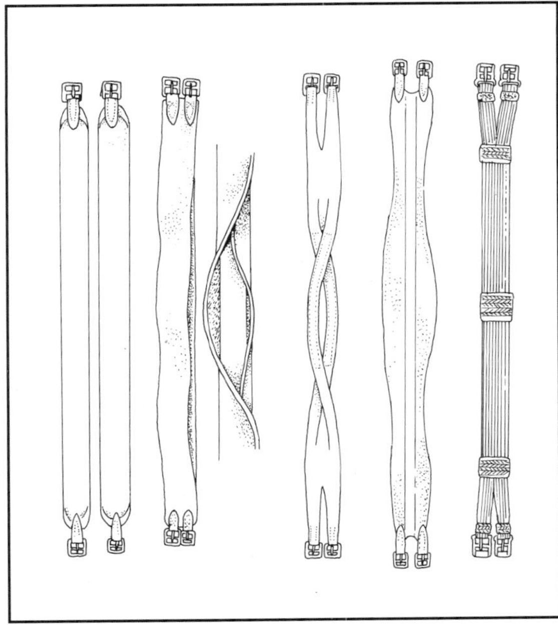

Types of girth, **from left**: a pair of webbing girths, Three-fold girth, Balding, Atherstone, nylon or string.

Stirrup-leathers

These are made from ordinary leather, raw-hide or buffalo hide. The latter two are very hard-wearing and largely unbreakable but are thicker than ordinary leather. Buffalo hide in particular stretches easily. Leathers should always be well cared for and the stitching checked regularly.

Stirrup-irons

They should be the right size for the rider, that is, about 2.5 cm (1 in) wider than the widest part of the boot. If they are too small, the foot could get caught in the stirrup; too big, and the rider's foot could slip right through. They should be of good quality metal, preferably stainless steel. With plated metal, the plating can chip or flake off. Solid

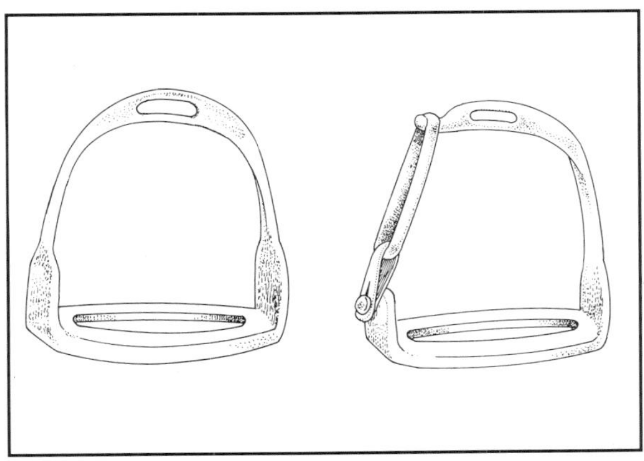

Stirrup-irons. **Left** Plain iron, and **right** safety iron.

nickel is too soft and brittle to be safe. The shape of the stirrup-iron is up to the rider and there are various styles on the market, but the standard iron is quite satisfactory. Safety stirrups have a rubber band instead of one metal side; it comes undone if, for any reason, the foot gets jammed in the stirrup. The drawback to these stirrups is that the rubber tends to become less elastic with use and the band can slip off unintentionally.

Pad saddles

With a first pony, particularly one which is small and round, a pad saddle is perfectly acceptable as a starting saddle. These saddles are made of felt, sometimes trimmed with leather, and have either no tree at all or just a part-tree forming a wither arch. The latter is better because it helps to keep the saddle in the right position. Pad saddles usually have their own webbing girth stitched to one side, which fastens by means of two buckles on the other side. If the saddle has a part-tree, it is usually fitted with proper stirrup-bars, but pad saddles with no tree may have D-rings instead of bars. These fittings should only be used with safety stirrups.

BUYING TACK

Always buy the best quality saddlery that you can afford. Bits are made from the same metal as stirrup-irons and the same standards apply to both. Stainless steel, hand-forged, is the best but it is also the most expensive.

Beware of some types of Asian saddles and bridles. The former may look perfectly all right, but inferior materials and workmanship in the parts of the saddle you cannot see could make the saddle dangerous. A second-hand English or German saddle is better value for money than a brand-new Asian import.

Some bridles, especially cheap ones, are made of Asian leather. Like the saddle, these may seem a good buy, but they tend to stretch with use, and quite noticeably when wet, which makes them dangerous.

Quite recently, bridles made from nylon webbing have been introduced. They are extremely practical for everyday use, but are not yet accepted in the show-ring. They are easy to care for because they can be washed. They can even be put in the washing-machine.

HEADCOLLAR AND LEAD-ROPE

A headcollar may be made of leather or nylon webbing, but in both cases the shape is the same. It consists of a noseband, held in place by a headpiece, with a section that passes under the cheek-bones and is linked to the noseband by a short strap. Wherever there is

Headcollar.

an intersection, a square or circular ring is used.

The nylon webbing headcollars are cheap and hard-wearing, and are the best buy for ponies, especially if your pony is difficult to catch and has to wear a headcollar while he is in the field. Leather headcollars look smart but they require much more care than the others and, of course, they are quite expensive.

Lead-ropes are made of jute or nylon, usually fitted with a clip so that it can be quickly fixed to the back of the headcollar. The cheapest lead-rope has a loop at one end, through which the free end of the rope passes after it has been put through the headcollar ring. The disadvantage of this method of fastening is that it can be very difficult to undo, especially if the rope is wet.

TACK CLEANING KIT

Your saddle and bridle will be safer and last much longer if you clean them properly. Few people manage to clean their tack *every* time they ride, but you should try to carry out this, for some reason most unwelcome, task at least once a week.

You will need a glycerine-based *saddle soap*, which comes in block form or in a tin, several sponges, a blunt knife and some leather oil. A few old matchsticks for removing saddle soap from buckle holes are useful.

Take both saddle and bridle apart and wash the bit and stirrup-irons in warm water. Wash the girth, unless it is made of leather, using a small nail-brush to remove the worst dirt, and hang it up to dry. Excess moisture should be removed with a towel. If you have a leather girth, clean it in the same way as the saddle.

Use the blunt knife to scrape off dried mud and the small blobs of grease, known as 'jockeys', which form on the lining of the saddle, the inside of the bridle and the end of the stirrup-leathers. A small, screwed-up pad of horse-hair is also effective at removing the 'jockeys'. With a damp sponge, well squeezed out, apply saddle soap to all leather surfaces, rubbing the soap in well. If the sponge is too wet, the soap will foam, which is good for cleaning but does not preserve the leather.

Once a month, apply a coating of leather oil to the tack after you have cleaned it, using a small brush, such as a soft paintbrush. The same oil should be put on any leather items of tack you are intending to store. It will keep the leather supple and prevent it from cracking.

The bit and stirrup-irons should be dried and buffed with a soft cloth, if they are stainless steel. Any other metal will need shining with metal polish, but polish should not be used on stainless steel as it dulls it.

Reassemble the saddle and bridle and put them carefully away.

SADDLE AND BRIDLE RACKS

It is possible to buy special racks for saddles and bridles, which can be put up in a cupboard, utility room or dry shed. They are specially designed to carry the tack without causing any damage. If you cannot afford to buy them ready-made, it is possible to make them.

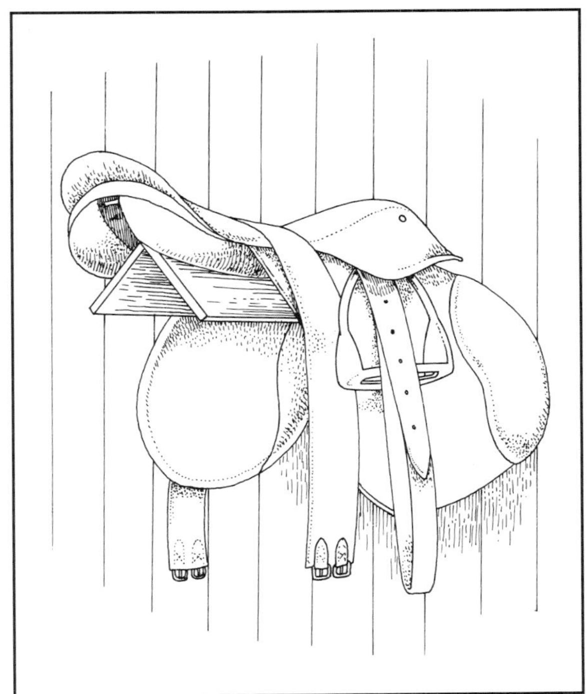

Saddle put up on a home-made rack.

A saddle rack should be shaped so that the saddle rests on its stuffing and not on the gullet. If you do have to put the saddle on the ground, stand it on the pommel, with the cantle leaning against the wall, protected from damage by the girth or a piece of cloth.

A piece of wood, cut from a log, or an old

1

2

3

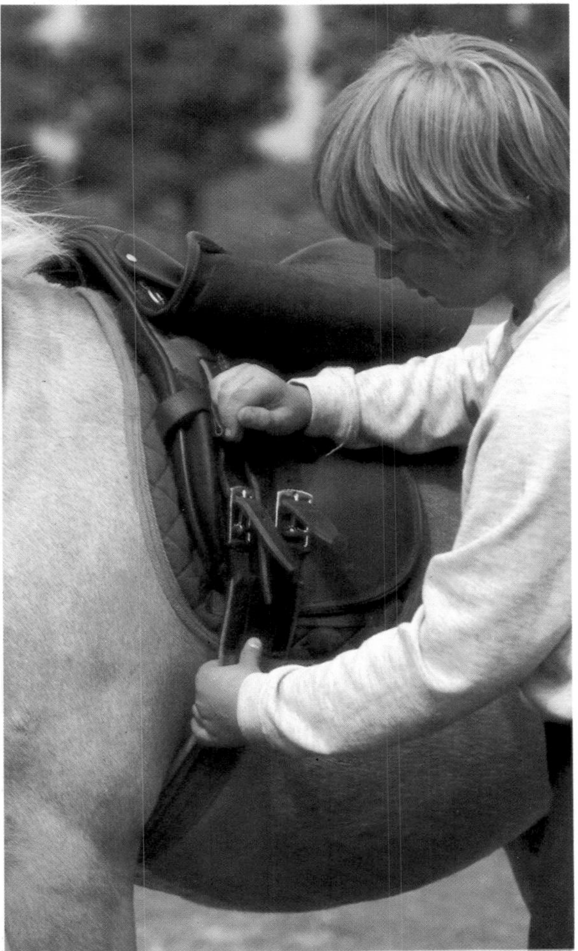

4

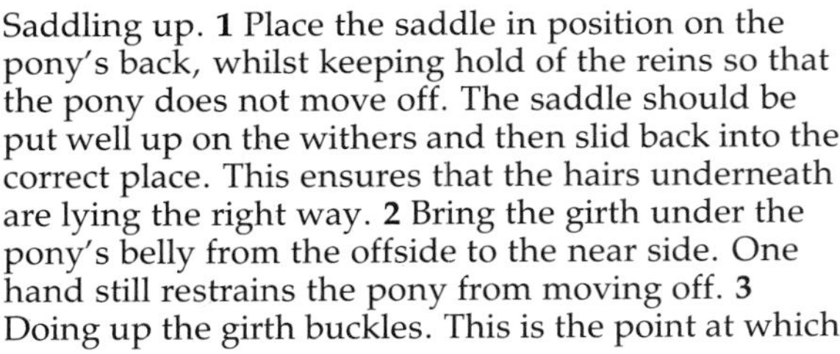

Saddling up. **1** Place the saddle in position on the pony's back, whilst keeping hold of the reins so that the pony does not move off. The saddle should be put well up on the withers and then slid back into the correct place. This ensures that the hairs underneath are lying the right way. **2** Bring the girth under the pony's belly from the offside to the near side. One hand still restrains the pony from moving off. **3** Doing up the girth buckles. This is the point at which a ticklish pony may get restive or put his ears back. Another awkward trick which many ponies adopt is to blow out their tummies so that it is difficult to get the buckles done up. If your pony does this, remember to tighten the girths a few minutes later when he has forgotten the trick. **4** Always run your hand down the inside of the girth to see that the hairs are lying straight and that no folds of skin are being pinched.

A saddle horse. Never store saddles on top of one another.

saddle soap tin screwed to the wall, are just the right shape for a bridle hook. Never hang your bridle on a coat hook or a nail – the weight of the bridle causes the leather to bend too sharply and eventually it can crack and break.

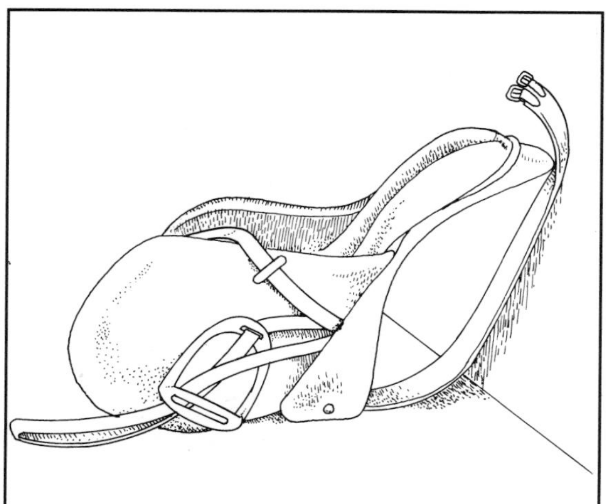

When a saddle is put on the ground, place it as shown, using the girth to protect the pommel and cantle.

GROOMING KIT

You can build up a grooming kit gradually or buy the items all in one go. Either way, you will need a box or bag to keep them in; preferably a light-weight box which is easy to carry. Some items are more important than others, so if you are planning to buy things gradually you should follow the order given here.

Hoof-pick This should be at the top of everyone's list because a pony's feet are so important. You use the hoof-pick to clean out the mud and small stones which collect in the sole and crevices of the hoof. The hooves should be picked out daily.

Body brush This is a soft, short-bristled brush which is used to remove dust and scurf from the coat and on the mane and tail.

Curry-comb A rubber curry-comb is useful for removing caked mud from the coat of a grass-kept pony. A metal curry-comb cleans the body brush.

Stable sponges These are ordinary foam rubber sponges used for cleaning the eyes, nose, muzzle and dock.

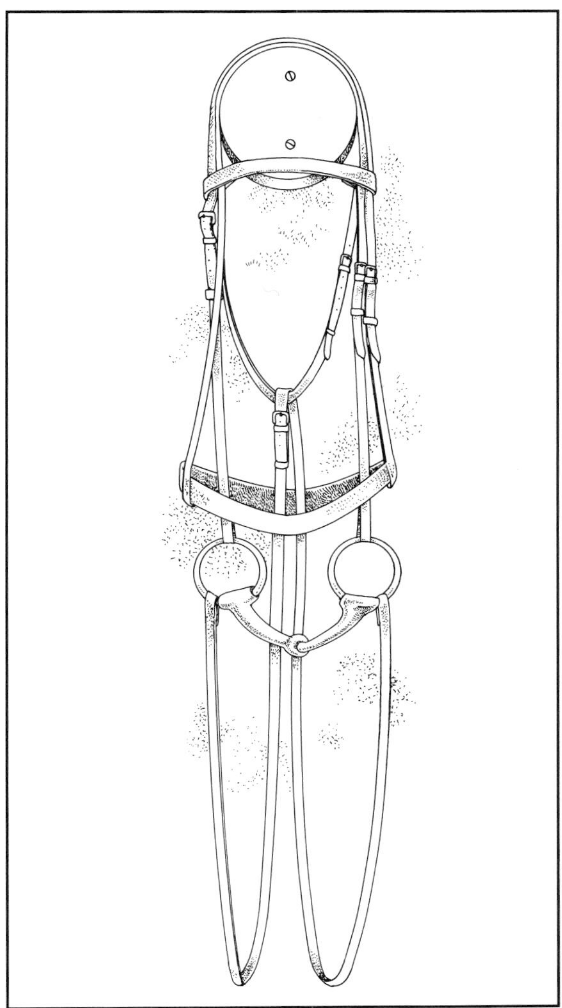

Snaffle bridle correctly put up.

Dandy-brush This is a coarse-bristled brush which can be used on a grass-kept pony to remove mud, dust and heavy dirt. It should not be used on the head or on the bony areas of the legs.

Water brush This has thick, soft bristles and is used to dampen the mane and tail when plaiting and to remove stains from the coat of a stable-kept horse.

Mane comb This is a broad, flat comb, made of metal or plastic, which is useful for dividing the mane when plaiting or in assisting with the pulling of hairs at the top of the tail. The object of the latter is to give the top of the tail a neat, tidy appearance, but it should never be carried out on a pony at grass because it deprives him of essential protection.

Hoof oil and brush The oil is applied to the outside of the hoof and the bulbs of the heels, to make the feet look smart and to help them if the horn is brittle or broken.

As you become more experienced, you will find yourself adding items to your grooming kit. A **stable-rubber**, for example, is like a big, linen tea-towel and it is used to give a final polish to a pony. An ordinary tea-towel is just as good as a cloth sold especially for the purpose. **Needles**, **plaiting bands** and **sewing thread** will be required when you have reached the stage of taking part in shows or of going hunting. A **sweat-scraper**, which is semi-circular in shape and has a rubber scraper attached, is used to remove sweat easily from a hot horse so that he will dry off quickly. It is also useful for removing shampoo or rinsing water from a pony which has been washed.

Shampoo This is another item which finds its way into most pony-owners' grooming kits. Special horse shampoos are available from saddlers and are better for your pony than your mother's expensively-scented shampoo from France. Washing-up liquid is very effective, as long as you remember to rinse it off thoroughly.

BUCKETS

You will need a number of buckets. One or two are just not enough. One bucket will be required to feed the pony from; another one or two will be needed for water. If you plan to feed sugar beet to your pony in the winter, you will want a bucket to soak it in. It is best to buy several inexpensive buckets, and immediately paint your name or your pony's name on them. This will prevent arguments if you are sharing the field with someone else's pony. All except the most expensive rubber buckets will deteriorate in time. They tend to become brittle when left outside in frosty weather, and ponies tread on them, kick them and sometimes even lie on them. All in all, a bucket has a rough life, so calculate the number you will need and add one more.

Pages 46–7 Bridling. **1** One hand holds the headpiece while the other gently guides the bit into the pony's mouth. **2** Once the bit is in, the headpiece is slid over the pony's ears. **3** The throat lash is brought to the nearside and **4** buckled. **5** Finally, the buckle of the cavesson noseband is fastened.

1

2

3

4

5

CHAPTER 5

Feeding and general care

Ponies do extremely well on a diet of grass. It is, after all, their natural food and they can cope quite comfortably with light work without any supplementary feeding of concentrates, such as oats or cubes. Summer grazing provides all the nutriments a pony needs; in winter, when there is little goodness in the grass, he should be given hay (grass which has been cut and dried at a time when its nutritional value is high).

A first pony is unlikely to be asked to do more work than a grass-only diet can sustain. This makes him reasonably inexpensive to keep. Although grass-fed ponies are healthy, they are not completely fit. They look bright-eyed and bouncy, but their fat is soft. Too much galloping will make them sweat and puff, but while you are still a novice your riding is unlikely to be too strenuous. It is only when your riding advances to the point that you want to enter for competitions, to ride a cross-country course, or to go out for a day's hunting, that your pony needs concentrated feed and a rigorous programme of exercise to build up his muscles and make him athletically fit.

The rules of feeding remain the same whether your pony is doing no more than a little light hacking, or hunting hard three or four days a week. It is the quantity and type of food which change.

A horse has a complicated digestive system, with a remarkably small stomach for his size. He needs to eat little and often, a programme which is easily maintained in the wild or when he is turned out into a field.

If you were to watch your pony throughout twenty-four hours, you would see that he spends long periods grazing, short periods resting, and that he intersperses these activities with an occasional burst of exercise, such as cantering around and bucking, and a few visits to the water trough.

A horse's digestive organs should always have some food in them, and grass or hay provides the necessary bulk.

First-time owners are often uncertain when to start giving a pony hay. In some countries, for example Britain, the winters can be very mild, and the cold weather may come early or late. It is difficult, therefore, to lay down a definite programme. The table opposite, however, offers guide-lines to the amounts which should be given daily.

The table does not take into account the short feeds which will help to see a hard-working grass-kept pony through the winter months. There are various types of grain – oats, barley, maize and so on – mixtures, cubes and other products, available from corn merchants, which will supplement the pony's winter hay ration. However, whichever you choose to give, and in what quantity, depends entirely on the amount of work your pony will be doing.

With a first pony and a novice rider, it is important to select the right ingredients for a short feed. Just because you have heard that oats are good for horses, do not assume that is what your pony must have. Some concentrates create energy and, unless your pony is able to work off that energy, you will be facing all sorts of problems. It is better to give your pony more hay than to introduce concentrates into his diet without taking expert advice.

	Size of pony		
	Under 12 hh	**12 to 13 hh**	**13 to 14 hh**
Early spring	2.2–3.2 kg (5–7 lb)	3.2–4.1 kg (7–9 lb)	4.1–5 kg (9–11 lb)
Late spring	No hay need be given unless your pony has a tendency to get very fat on grass. Then you should, if possible, put him in a stable for three to four hours with a small haynet.		
Summer	No hay	No hay	No hay
Early autumn	Start offering a small quantity of hay if the weather is cold or wet. If the hay is not eaten by the next day, leave for a week, then try again.		
Late autumn	Gradually increase the amount of hay.		
Winter	2.2–4.5 kg (5–10 lb)	4.5–5.4 kg (10–12 lb)	5.4–6.8 kg (12–15 lb)

A guide to the amount of hay that should be fed daily to a grass-kept pony.

HAY

There are several types of hay, depending on the pasture that it is made from. In the UK there are three types – seed, meadow and clover – of which the first two are the best for horses. In the USA, alfalfa hay is the most commonly available.

Seed hay is hay grown from selected seeds, usually such grasses as Cocksfoot, Timothy, Crested Dogs-tail, and Perennial and Italian Rye-grasses. Sometimes red and white clover is added. If it has been properly sown and cared for and harvested at the right time – between the flowering and seeding stages – it will be nutritious without being overheating.

Meadow hay comes from permanent meadows and should contain all or some of the grasses mentioned above. It may also contain perennial weeds such as docks, dandelions, buttercups and thistles. This does not matter very much as long as they do not make up the bulk of the contents. Like seed hay, it should have been harvested at the proper time and, when new, will be greenish in colour and soft to the touch. As it grows older, the colour fades.

Clover hay is dark in colour, rather brittle and very sweet-smelling. It is grown from seed-sown clovers and is extremely nutritious, particularly for cattle. However, it is too rich for horses and ponies, and should never be offered to ponies except in small quantities mixed with another type of hay.

Alfalfa is made from lucerne and is particularly common in the USA. It is a protein-rich food, much richer than meadow hay, and smaller quantities would be needed to keep a pony fit and well. Late-cut alfalfa can be woody, and a pony might take some time to get used to it. It is dustier than ordinary hay and needs to be sprinkled with water before being offered to horses. Cubes or pellets made from alfalfa are richer than hay is in vitamin A and calcium.

In addition, you may come across *Horsehage*, the proprietary name for a guaranteed dust-free form of dried grass, which is supplied vacuum-packaged in bags. It is ideal for horses which suffer from chronic respiratory problems or allergies to ordinary hay.

Good quality hay smells pleasant and is reasonably free from dust. If possible, hay should be between six and eighteen months old before being given to horses. This means that some of the previous season's crop should be saved to start off the following winter. As a general rule, hay taken from the field in mid-summer should not be fed to ponies until the following mid-winter. The reason for this is that new hay still has some chemical changes to go through while in store, before it becomes easy to digest.

Never buy hay which is yellow, blackish, wet or mouldy, and if, because your storage conditions are not very good, your hay has reached this state by the end of the winter, it is better to scrap the remaining bales and buy in some more.

When and where you buy your hay depends on the amount of storage space you have. A dry shed or barn with a concrete floor is the ideal place to store hay, and it will keep well if the stack stands on a layer of pallets. One pony will consume approximately one tonne (one ton) of hay during the winter. This is about fifty bales (each bale some 25.4 kg (56 lb), or quite a large stack. You are lucky indeed if you have room to store a whole winter's supply because it means that you can buy your hay 'off the field', which is usually the cheapest way of buying it. Buying off the field means that you arrange with a local farmer to take the amount of hay you think you will need straight from the field where it is being harvested. You may have to collect it yourself, or for a small extra fee the farmer might deliver the load to you. His willingness to do this depends on how advanced he is with the harvest, and on the weather. If he still has several fields to tackle, he may say that he cannot spare the time.

The collection of hay from the field is not a job that can be postponed. If the opportunity of buying the hay comes along on a Monday or Tuesday, it is very risky to wait until the following weekend. The fine weather may break, and heavy rain will ruin the hay. Better to miss a ride or the chance to go swimming, and set off there and then. Persuade your parents to make several journeys with the car, if necessary, or borrow a small lorry or a horse-trailer. A trailer, incidentally, can carry between thirty and forty bales, but you will need as many strong people to help you as you can muster.

If you do not have enough storage space to buy hay in bulk, you will have to buy hay as you need it. Most people can find the space to store six or eight bales at a time and this represents about two weeks supply for your pony. If you can find a supplier who will sell you enough for the winter but allow you to pick up the hay when you need it, you will probably not have to pay very much more per bale than buying 'off the field'. However, if you have to buy hay in very small quantities, you will find that the price tends to rise as the winter goes on, and especially if the spring is wet or prolonged and hay supplies become hard to get. Bought this way, it can also vary considerably in quality.

Never forget that hay is the most important winter food that you can give your pony. Try to get good quality hay, and do not be mean in the amount you give. Avoid 'bargain offers', especially at the end of the winter. If hay is advertised at a suspiciously cheap price, the likelihood is that it has deteriorated while in store; perhaps it was not properly dried, and much of it will not only be unfit to eat, but could be harmful. A hungry pony will eat poor hay but it will do him little good.

THE DAILY FEEDING ROUTINE: WINTER

Ponies should be given hay at the same time each day. No doubt the best time is straight after school and before it has grown dark. You can provide the hay in a haynet or put it straight on the ground. There are advantages and drawbacks to both methods.

A haynet is the least wasteful. You simply stuff the net full of hay, pull the drawstring tight and tie it to a convenient fence-rail or post or to a tree. This method keeps the hay clear of mud, and very little will be trampled underfoot. However, you must make absolutely certain that the net is tied high enough to clear the ground even when it is half-empty, and an empty haynet hangs much lower than a full one. Unless its anchoring point is really secure – such as a tree – the tugging of the pony as he pulls out each mouthful can put a strain on the post or rail, which may eventually loosen it. You can then end up with an insecure fence. The haynet should always be tied with a quick-release knot.

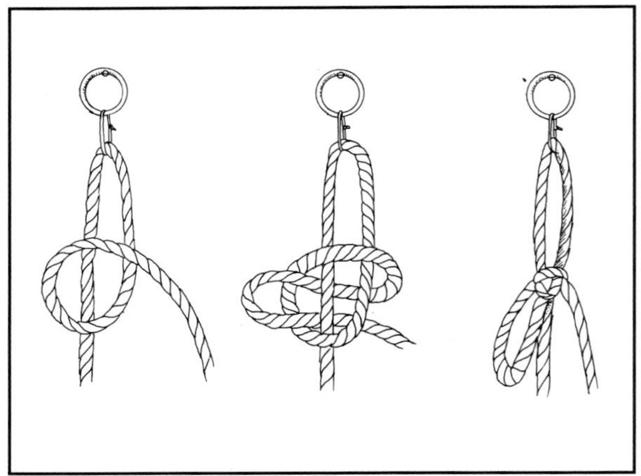

The stages of tying a quick-release knot.

Opposite Always use a body brush on a pony's head, forelock and around his ears.

Hay placed on the ground is the most natural method for a pony to feed. However, some of the hay will be wasted, especially if the ground is wet or poached. This is probably the best method if there are several ponies in the field. Place the hay in piles well apart from one another to keep quarrelling to a minimum, and always add an extra pile to

give shy ponies the chance to eat their fill. Bossy ponies seem to delight in moving from one pile to another, forcing the others to move on.

Ponies soon learn when to expect your arrival with their food and will be waiting for you. If you are late, they will get restless and may start kicking and biting. So work out a routine that fits into the rest of your activities and stick to it.

A visit once a day is usually sufficient. If the weather is frosty or there is snow on the ground, you should go twice. A small feed of hay on frosty mornings is beneficial. In any case, you should visit the field early to break the ice on the water trough. During long spells of icy weather, you may have to bring fresh water to the field in buckets. At this time of the year, it is particularly important to keep the trough well filled – each time you remove chunks of ice, you are lowering the water level, and if the hose or pipe which supplies the water is exposed, it can freeze solid.

During your visit to the field, always check your pony over carefully. Look particularly at his feet. On hard, frozen ground, an unshod pony's hooves may crack or split or he may suffer from a bruised sole or heels. There is less chance of any of these problems happening if the pony is shod. When there is snow on the ground, the snow can collect in the foot and form a hard ball of ice, a common reason for bruising. The best way of ensuring that the snow does not collect is to smear the sole of the foot with motor grease.

When the weather is wet, the ground will get soggy and poached. Watch out for cracked heels or mud fever, which are both due to an infection contracted by getting the legs and feet caked with mud. The symptoms are sore patches on the legs and belly or deep cracks in the heels. The infection can be prevented by smearing petroleum jelly around the heels and over the pastern and fetlock joint. Ponies, with plenty of hair on the legs and around the fetlocks, are less likely to suffer from the condition than horses.

THE DAILY FEEDING ROUTINE: SUMMER

Even though you are not feeding your pony in summer, you should visit him every day. As the evenings grow lighter you will be able to ride him more often. Remember, however, that he is in soft condition, so do not gallop him about too much. Always return from a ride quietly, giving him a chance to cool down before you turn him out into the field.

Keep his water trough clean. In hot weather, algae can form very quickly, turning the water green and slimy. The trough will need a once-a-week scrubbing and hosing out, before being refilled with fresh water.

Flies can be a problem, particularly at dusk. Shade is very necessary to ponies. Use a proprietary fly-repellent on the face and body. A fly fringe, which fits on to the headcollar like a browband, is good at keeping flies away from the pony's eyes. A gauze fly-mask which fits over his ears and fastens under the cheek-bones is also effective, and ponies rarely object to wearing them.

GROOMING

The purpose of grooming is to stimulate the skin, to remove mud and loose hairs from the coat, and to make the pony look clean and tidy. There is no need to groom the pony if you are not intending to ride him, and you should never be too vigorous in your attentions to a pony which lives out.

The reason for this is that the pony's coat is his principal means of keeping warm and dry. When you run your hand through a pony's coat, you will notice a greasy deposit on your fingers. The same greasy deposit gets on the tack and on your boots. This is a natural grease which helps to keep your pony waterproof. A pony's winter coat is made up of short, thick hairs covered by a thatch of longer hairs. The short, thick hairs provide insulation, the longer ones repel rain-water. In dry, cold weather, the pony looks like a shaggy bear, quite different from the shiny, sleek creature of the summer months. His coat is well designed to keep out the worst of the weather. Even his mane and tail take on a bushy look.

In winter, therefore, confine your grooming simply to removing caked-on mud, and the tangles from his mane and tail. The best tools for this purpose are a rubber curry-comb or stiff-bristled dandy-brush for the mud, and the body brush for the mane and tail. Use a hoof-pick to clean out the underside of his hooves. The hoof-pick, in fact, is the only item you should use every day.

In spring, your pony will start to lose his winter coat. This is a very tedious time of the

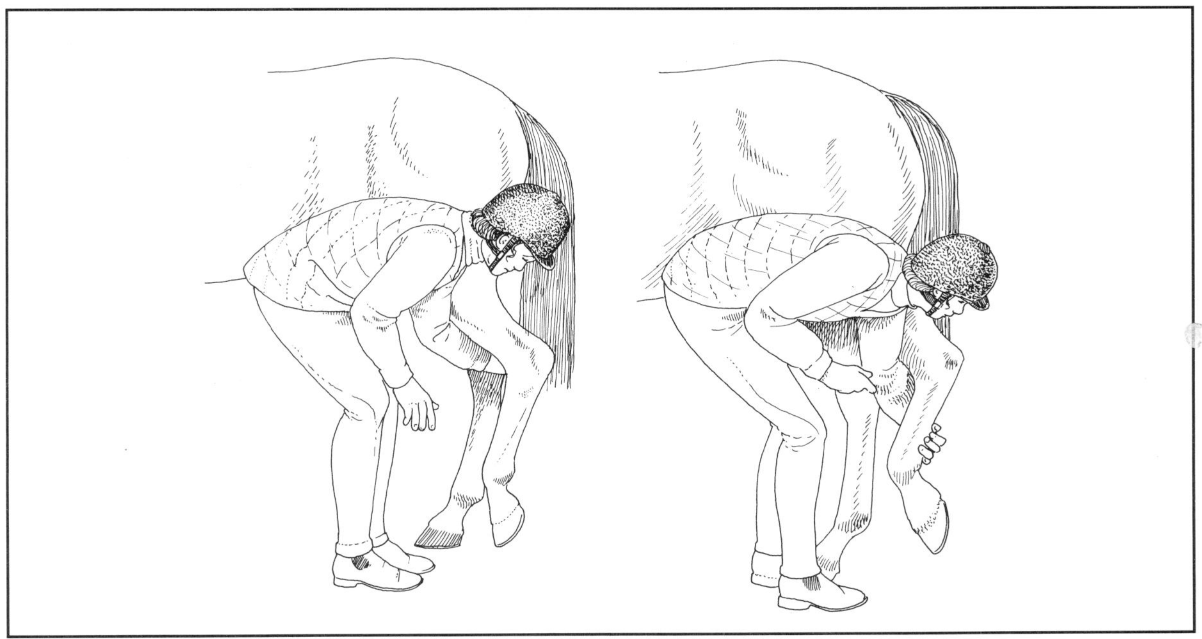

Picking up a hind leg. Stand to one side and run your inside hand down the pony's leg from hock to fetlock. Grasp the fetlock and gently pull the foot upwards.

year both for him and you, as the process of losing his coat will make him feel itchy and will cover you, whenever you ride, with quantities of loose hairs. You can help to speed the transition from winter to summer coat by grooming him regularly, making a big effort to get rid of the clumps of matted loose hair which tend to form on his chest and belly and between his legs.

Gradually, however, the summer coat emerges. Now the woolly bear resembles a pony once again. The summer coat is short and has a healthy sheen. There will still be a layer of grease on the pony's skin, necessary to protect him against summer rain, and you may well raise a cloud of dust when you pat the pony. Any loose bits of grass and surface dust should be removed with the body brush, and on smart occasions, a going-over with a dampened water brush will help to stop the dust from flying about. Now is the time to trim the hair from his fetlocks – it will grow again in readiness for the winter. Always remember to clean out his feet and use damp sponges to wipe his eyes, nostrils, muzzle and dock.

At the end of the summer, the winter coat starts to grow. The first signs are a loosening of the short hairs and the disappearance of the sheen. Gradually, you become aware that the pony is taking on a furry look once more. Now you should be more careful than ever not to remove too much grease when you groom.

CARE OF THE FEET

Very few people nowadays are able to take their ponies to the forge and most rely on the farrier visiting them. Farriers travel round with the necessary equipment: portable anvils, a collection of shoes and nails, and sometimes even a portable brazier.

If the farrier brings his own fire, or you can call at a forge, your pony can be hot-shod in the traditional way. This means that the farrier can hold the hot shoe to the pony's foot and make any necessary adjustments to its size and shape.

Cold-shoeing, provided it is carried out by a farrier who knows his job, is perfectly satisfactory. If it is the first time the farrier has shod your pony, ask him to look at the pony's feet and take the measurements himself. He will then make the shoes at his forge and return to put them on. If he asks you to give him details of the shoe sizes, you should measure across the widest part of the pony's existing shoes and again from heel to toe.

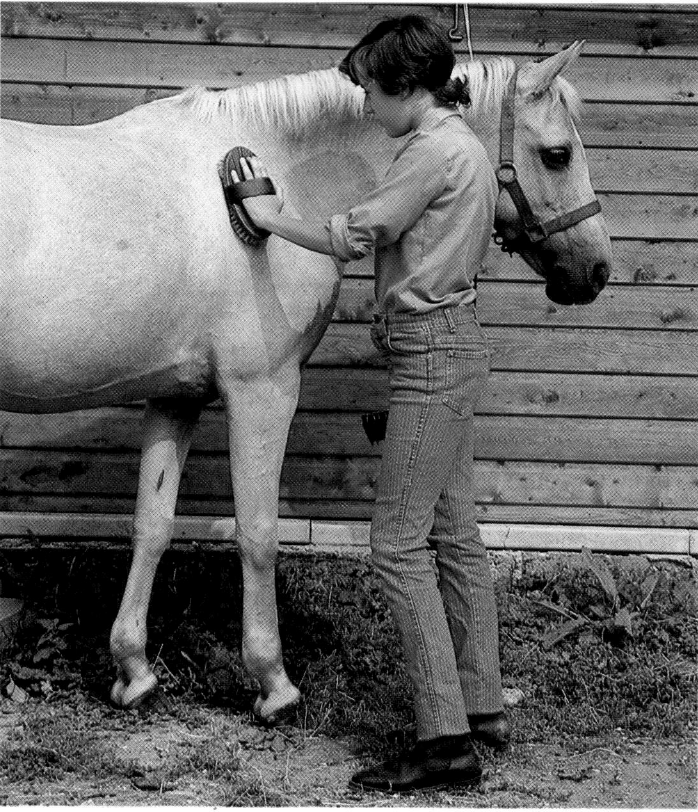

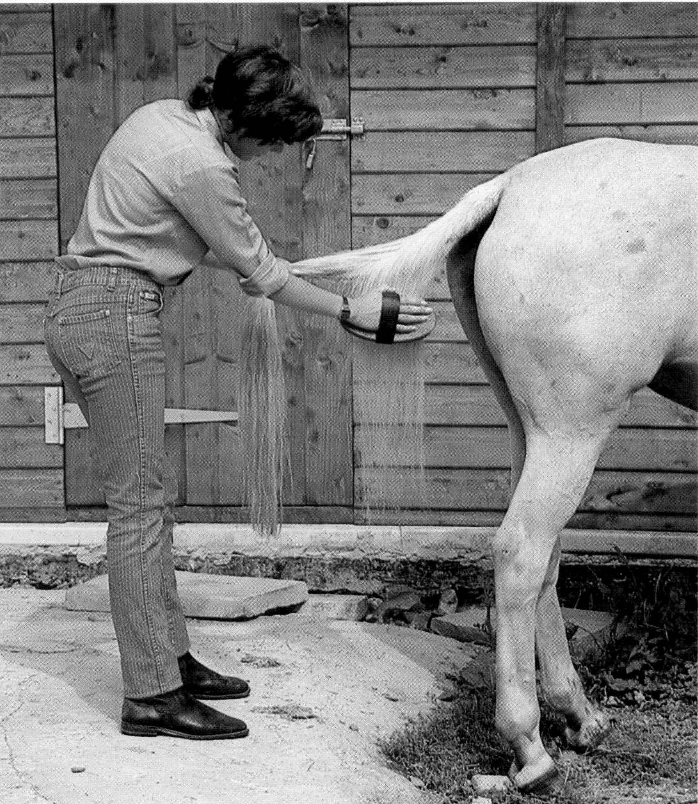

Above Grooming the nearside **left**, and the offside **right**. Note that you always use the right hand on the near side, and the left hand on the offside, regardless of whether you are right-handed or left-handed.

Left Grooming the tail. Use a body brush, and brush a small section at a time.

Below Remember to sponge the nostrils, and around the mouth and eyes.

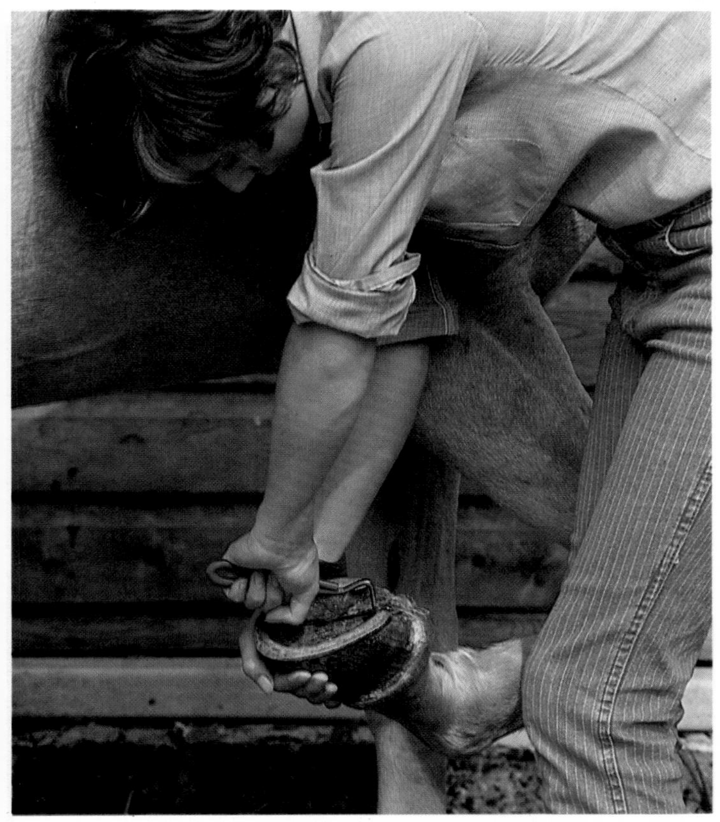

Above Picking out the front and hind hooves. Always stand close to the pony's body, and hold the hoof in the inside hand.

Left and below To smarten up your pony's feet for a show or special occasion, you can oil the heels and the walls of the hooves. Use a soft brush and apply the oil liberally. Never kneel on the ground beside a pony's feet; crouch beside him, so that you can move out of the way quickly if he stamps his foot or kicks out.

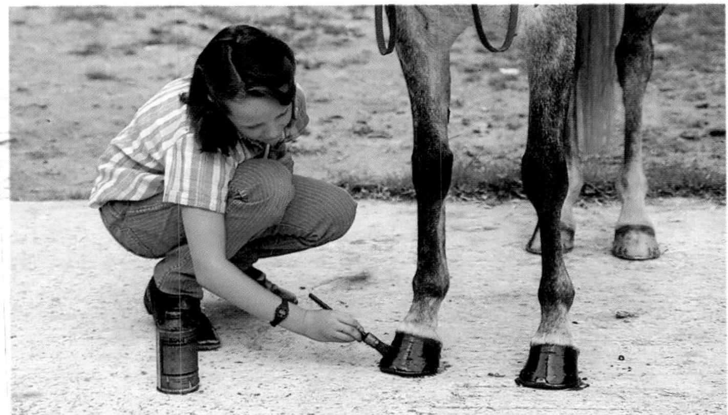

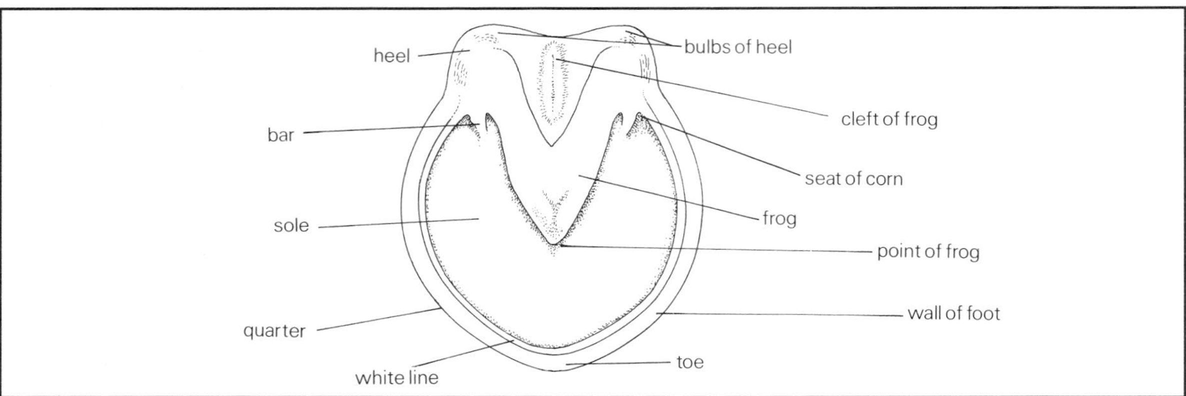

The parts of the foot.

After the first shoeing, the farrier will keep a record of your pony's requirements.

Most farriers charge at a rate of so much per set of shoes, plus travelling expenses and VAT. Where more than one pony is to be shod, travelling expenses can be shared. Because a pony's feet are so important, it is better to pay more for the services of a really reputable farrier than risk ruining your pony's feet by going to a cut-price, incompetent one.

Some ponies are heavier on their shoes than others, and only experience will tell you how often your pony needs shoeing. Examine the shoes each time you pick out the pony's feet. Examine the clenches: the part of the nail that emerges through the wall of the hoof, is twisted off and hammered down. As the shoes wear, the clenches may rise. As the hoof grows, it may overgrow the shoe. In time, parts of the shoe wear thin, and sometimes a shoe works loose. You should always be on the look-out for tell-tale signs and be ready to make your appointment with the farrier.

His first task is to remove the old shoes. This he does by hammering up the clenches and levering the shoe off with a pair of pincers. He will then trim away the overgrown horn, levelling the foot so that, even when the shoe is in place, the frog, which absorbs jar and helps to stop the pony from slipping, will come in contact with the ground. He tests the new shoe against the foot and may make a few minor adjustments to it, using his hammer and anvil.

Once satisfied, he fixes the shoe in place with nails. Herein lies much of the skill of the farrier. The wall of the hoof is insensitive, and it will not hurt the pony to have nails driven into this part. The point of each nail emerges higher up on the outside of the hoof. If the farrier is careless, he can place the nail too close to the sensitive inside of the sole, which will quickly cause lameness, or too close to the outside, which will cause part of the hoof to break away and the shoe to be loosened.

When all the nails (usually seven) are hammered home, the farrier twists off their points and hammers over the ends, or clenches. Finally, he rasps the horn smooth.

Ponies who do little roadwork may not need new shoes each time the farrier calls. Unless the shoes are badly worn, he may decide to trim the feet and replace the old shoes. These are known as removes and the charge is less than for supplying new shoes. Be guided by your farrier's advice, and if your pony has any problems with his feet talk them over with him. Special shoes may, in some cases, counteract the effects of poor conformation or clumsy leg action.

It is difficult to be definite about how often your pony should need shoeing. A visit from the farrier may be necessary at intervals of anything from four weeks to three months, depending on how much work the pony has to do and how quickly his feet grow.

CHAPTER 6

Clothing for rider and pony

Riding clothes are designed to be practical and smart, but above all to give the rider protection in the event of an accident. Most people know that, for safety's sake, they should always wear a proper riding hat. But did you know that it is just as important to wear the correct type of shoes or boots?

THE RIDER'S CLOTHING

Safety and comfort are the two most important elements in the choice of riding clothes.

Hats

It may surprise many people to know that riding is one of the most dangerous of all sports: in Britain, for example, it has the highest number of fatalities per year. And of all injuries sustained in riding accidents, around two-thirds are suffered by the head.

A hard hat, therefore, is essential. It should be made to a standard approved by the national body governing safety standards. (In the UK this is the British Standards Institution, and their approved products bear a label with the well-known BSI 'kite' mark.)

In 1984, the BSI, together with manufacturers and leading members of the horse world, met together to produce a riding hat with a higher degree of safety than before. The result was the new British Standard No 6473, which replaced the old BS 3686.

The new standard means that the hat has a greater resistance to impact than before and that it must be so fitted that it will stay in place at all times.

To achieve this, it has a high-quality shell, flexible peak, impact-absorbing ventilation button, and a urethane shell liner and self-conforming head pad replacing the drawstring system. The old drawstring, which should always have been pulled tight enough to leave a cushion of air between the top of the hat and the head, was far too often left undone or was so slackly tied that it was useless. In the new hat, the shock-absorbing head pad is built in.

Finally, the hat has a specially developed three point harness which can be used with or without a chin cup.

In appearance, the hat is little different from earlier hats. It is velvet-covered and available in various colours. Most people prefer black, navy blue or dark brown. As before, it is trimmed with a ribbon bow at the back, but unless you are the child of a farmer or a hunt servant, you should cut off the ribbons or fold them under and stitch them down.

Pony Club members should also be aware of a new Pony Club ruling. This states that from 1 January, 1986, every competitor in Pony Club area competitions must wear a jockey skull-cap, BS 4472. Anyone wearing any other type of hat will not be allowed to take part.

You may already possess a suitable skull-cap, especially if you enter cross-country events and hunter trials. The skull-cap – or crash cap – has a glass fibre shell, and lightweight silk covers in different colours can be bought for it. It is held on by means of a chin harness. You should always take trouble to buy a crash hat that fits you properly, and a well-fitting hat is not uncomfortable.

If you have a bad fall, or your hat receives a blow or kick, you should have the hat examined by an expert before continuing to use it. A damaged hat *must* be replaced.

Boots

Whatever type of footwear you choose, it must have a clearly defined heel. The heel prevents your foot from slipping through the stirrup-iron and perhaps getting jammed if you fall. For this reason flat-soled shoes, such as gymshoes and trainers, are dangerous for riding. Wellington boots are also unsuitable because they are wider than riding boots would be, and may get caught in the stirrup-iron.

For young children, jodhpur boots are sensible, comfortable and hard-wearing. They protect the ankle from being rubbed by the stirrup-iron, and they have a proper heel. They are usually black or brown and have either an elasticated gusset or a strap and buckle fastening.

Rubber, knee-length riding boots are a recent innovation and can be worn over jodhpurs or with conventional breeches. They are shaped to the leg and the top is cut away slightly on the inside. They are easy to keep clean because mud and grease can be sponged off. Before buying a pair, however, try them not only for foot comfort but also for length. Some are quite high and can cut into the back of the knee when the leg is bent.

They are not a substitute for wellington boots because the sole is not grooved and gives little grip when you are walking in mud.

Jodhpurs

A pair of stretch jodhpurs are comfortable and practical, and they wash easily. If made from two-way stretch material, they give complete freedom of movement. Most riders have more than one pair, keeping light-coloured ones (white, yellow, cream or fawn) for important occasions and using dark-coloured ones (dark brown or dark green) for everyday use. Stretch denim jodhpurs are also popular for general wear.

Always try on jodhpurs before you buy them as, to be effective, the strappings must be in the right place. The strappings are those extra pieces which line the inside of the knee and half-way down the calf, preventing chafing or pinching from the stirrup-leathers. On very expensive jodhpurs and breeches, the strappings are made of soft suede, but this means that they have to be dry-cleaned.

Ordinary denim jeans or cotton trousers can be used for casual riding, but they give less protection to the inside of the leg.

Jackets

A riding jacket is slightly waisted, and has a flared skirt and one or two slits at the back. The shape ensures that it hangs properly and looks smart when the wearer is in the saddle. For young children, a tweed jacket is suitable for all occasions. However, later on, if you enter showing classes, you will need a black, brown or navy blue showing jacket as well. Showing jackets usually have a velvet collar. In jumping classes at a show, even on a hot day, the judge will often insist on your wearing a jacket. This is because it provides some protection for your arms, shoulders and back should you be unlucky enough to fall off.

For everyday riding, there is no need to wear a jacket as a sweat-shirt and anorak, or jersey and quilted waistcoat, are comfortable and practical.

Shirt and tie

These are necessary only when you are showing or jumping. The shirt should be a plain pale colour, such as white, blue, fawn or yellow, and the tie should also be plain coloured. A Pony Club tie, with its distinctive pale blue, gold and purple stripes, is always correct.

Gloves

String gloves, leather gloves, or gloves with leather palms will help you to grip the reins on a wet day. They are always part of a showing outfit whatever the weather. Gloves tend to get lost easily so it is wise to have a spare pair.

Hair

Hair should always be tidy. Long hair can be plaited in one or two plaits; medium-length or short hair needs a hairnet to keep it in place. Ear-rings should never be worn while riding, nor should other forms of jewelry except a Pony Club or similar badge.

THE PONY'S CLOTHING

If you look round a saddler's shop or flick through the advertising pages of a horse magazine, you could be forgiven for wondering whether your pony is an animal or a fashion model. There are all manner of rugs in many different materials, brightly-coloured bandages, items in felt, leather and rubber to protect the pony's legs, waterproof sheets to

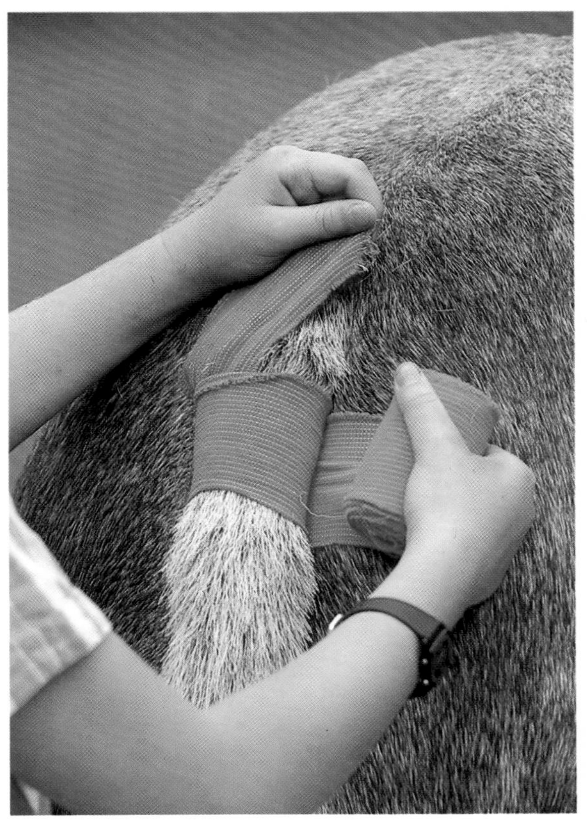

2

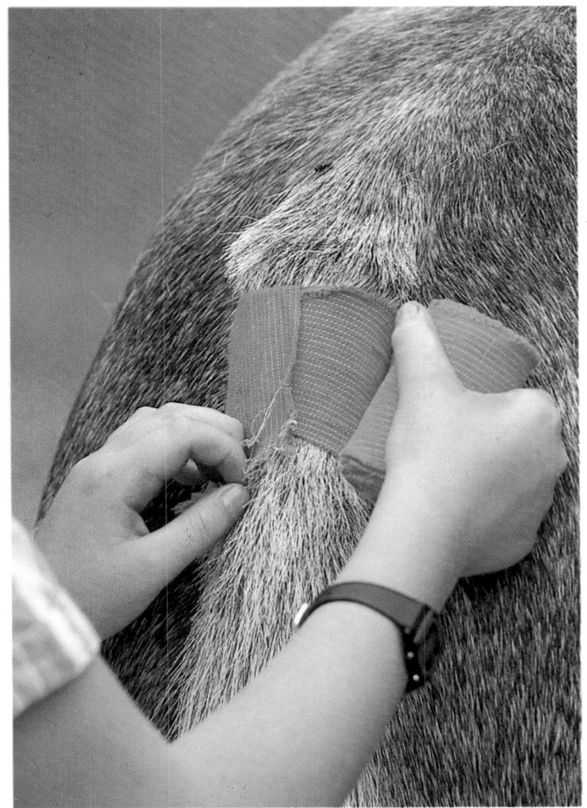

3

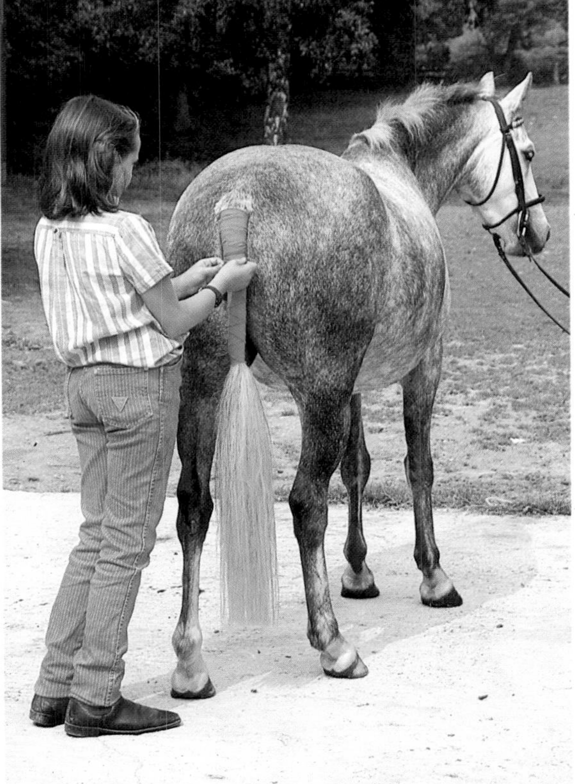

Putting on a tail bandage. **1** Start by holding the end against the top of the tail and take a turn round the tail to keep the end in position. **2** Fold over the projecting end and carry on winding, down to the end of the dock and back up again. **3** Finish off by tying the tapes round the tail, neatly and securely but not too tightly.

keep off the rain, furry numnahs to go under the saddle, and so on.

None of these things is necessary for a novice rider with a grass-kept pony. Nature has given him a perfectly adequate fur rug of his own, which has all the necessary warmth-giving and waterproofing qualities. Provided he can exercise himself properly and has plenty of fresh water and food, he can cope with all forms of weather and remain bright-eyed and healthy.

Remember that all native breeds of pony are hardy and tough by nature. What such a pony does *not* need is a New Zealand rug, and you should resist the temptation to buy him one. A New Zealand rug is an outdoor rug designed to keep a *clipped* horse warm and dry when he is running loose in a field. It is cut to a special shape and fitted with straps and sometimes a surcingle, in order that it will stay in place even when the horse rolls.

Unfortunately, many pony-owners believe that an unclipped pony also needs a New Zealand rug. In consequence, at the first sign of bad weather in the autumn, the poor pony is bundled into his winter clothing and has to suffer the discomfort of wearing it for the next six months. Yet the disadvantages of such a rug on a pony with a full winter coat are numerous.

First of all, it flattens the coat, reducing its natural insulation. Secondly, it tends to impede the pony's movements, making it more difficult for him to move about in order to keep warm. Thirdly, on mild days, it can make the pony too hot, so that he starts to sweat. As the sweat cools, his body gets clammy and he can easily catch cold.

A New Zealand rug, even if it fits well, can chafe, particularly on the points of the shoulders and over the withers. The leg straps, where they pass between the hind legs, may also rub. At least twice a day, the pony must be caught and the rug checked to see that it has not slipped.

Far better, therefore, to leave your pony with his own natural coat.

Tail bandage

This is likely to be the only item of clothing a first pony will need. You use it to make the hairs at the top of the tail stay in place. It is also part of the protective clothing that a pony wears when he is travelling. A tail bandage is made of stockinette or crepe and is rolled up from the tape end, with the sewn side of the tape inwards.

To put on a tail bandage, start by dampening the top of the tail slightly with the water brush. Unroll about 25 cm (10 in) of the bandage; pass this underneath the tail as high up as it will go. Hold the free end firmly in place at the root of the tail with one hand; with the other hand, unroll the bandage over the free end, and then make one complete turn of the tail. Fold down the loose end and take a turn over it and round the tail, slightly higher than the first turn. Continue to unroll the bandage round the tail, moving downwards and overlapping the turns as you go. Stop just short of the end of the tail bone and tie the tapes securely, but not too tightly.

Never wet the bandage before you put it on, in case it shrinks and injures the tail, nor leave a tail bandage on all night. If it is tight enough to stay in place for the whole night it is too tight, and could interfere with the circulation and harm the tail.

To remove a tail bandage, undo the tapes, then take hold of the bandage at the top of the tail and, using both hands, slide it downwards and off the tail in one quick movement.

CHAPTER 7

Schooling and jumping

The secret of good, sympathetic riding lies in achieving balance and harmony. You must aim to remain in perfect balance with your pony's movements, not only at each of the different paces, but also during transitions (the changes from one pace to another). This will enable you to give clear instructions to the pony (through the use of the aids) and will enable the pony to respond to them correctly, thereby keeping you and the pony in harmony.

BALANCE

When you first learned to ride, your instructor will have stressed the importance of sitting 'square', with your hips parallel to the pony's quarters and your shoulders parallel to his shoulders, while you keep looking

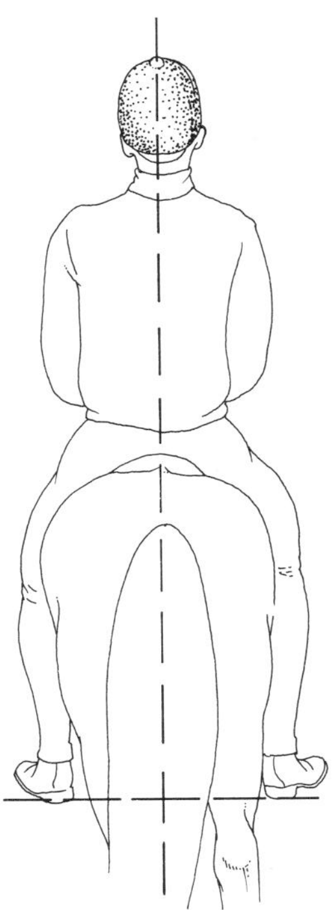

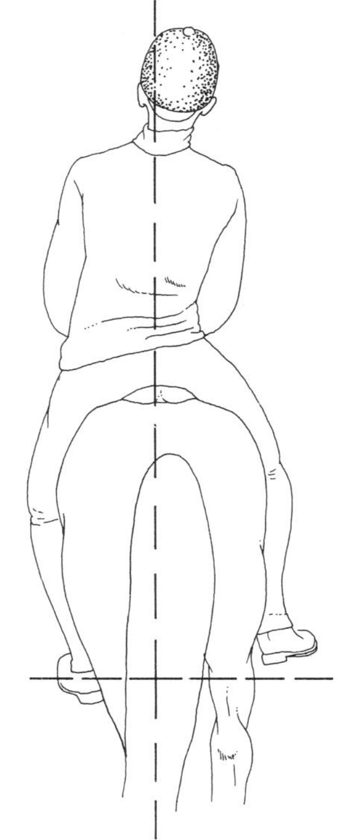

A square seat is one of the first requisites of a balanced seat. If your seat is crooked, **right**, the pony cannot balance himself properly with the weight of his rider.

ahead in the direction in which you are going. In this position you remain balanced on the pony.

The pony also has to learn how to balance himself, when carrying the weight of a rider. He must use his muscles correctly: his weight should be on his hind legs, he should carry his head and neck in a natural position, and give no resistance to the bit.

The rider must create forward movement, called *impulsion*, through the use of the lower leg and seat (see page 63). This gives the impression of energy even at a walk. There must be no sign of the pony dragging his feet. He should be alert and supple, his hind legs active and his paces rhythmic.

Opposite A nice position on a pony. Note the straight line formed by the rein and the rider's fore-arm.

Three diagrams showing how the rider's position has to change with the pony's paces in order to keep the rider's centre of gravity in balance with the pony's. **Top left**, at a walk; **top right**, at a gallop; **bottom**, jumping.

THE AIDS

These are the means by which the rider tells the pony what to do. They should always be clear and should only be repeated if the pony does not respond immediately. There are two kinds of aids. The voice, body, legs and hands are *natural aids.* Whips and spurs are *artificial aids*. Artificial aids are used only to emphasize the natural aids.

The voice The voice encourages, calms, praises and occasionally scolds the pony. With a young or unschooled pony, the voice can be used to instruct. Phrases like 'walk on', 'halt', 'trot' or 'steady' will help to reinforce the signals given by the legs or hands. The voice, however, should not be used during a dressage test.

The body This can pass information to the pony by its movement; in addition the muscles of the seat help to create impulsion. The rider, however, should always remain in balance.

The legs While the thigh muscles stay relaxed and the hip and knee joints stay supple, the lower part of the leg is used to give definite signals. A short, sharp application of pressure by the inside leg asks for impulsion. Increased pressure on one side makes the pony bend correctly when moving in a circle or curve. A correct bend occurs when the pony's body follows the line of the curve without deviating or bending away from it.

The hindquarters are controlled by the outside lower leg. Pressure behind the girth, quickly but firmly applied, with the leg returning immediately to its normal position, asks the pony to canter. Continuous pressure controls the direction of the hindquarters and should cease once the movement has been correctly carried out.

The hands The hands indicate direction and control the pony's speed. Quick pressure of the inside hand, followed by relaxation of the fingers indicates direction. The outside hand repeats this movement to regulate the pace.

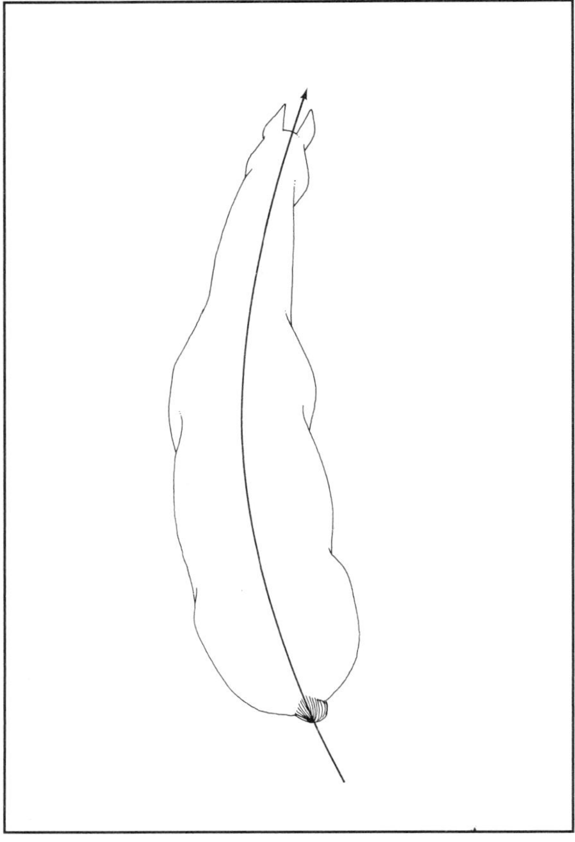

A pony is said to be bending correctly when his body follows the direction of the curve and his hind feet follow the tracks of the front feet.

Aids to turning the pony. **Left** The rider's hand is brought sideways and forwards, leading the pony in a wide arc. **Right** The rider's legs and seat control forward movement and the hindquarters while pressure on the inside rein shows the pony which way to go.

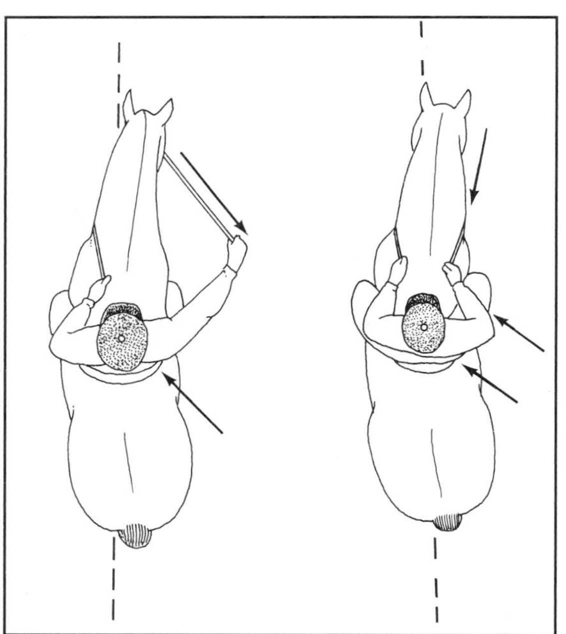

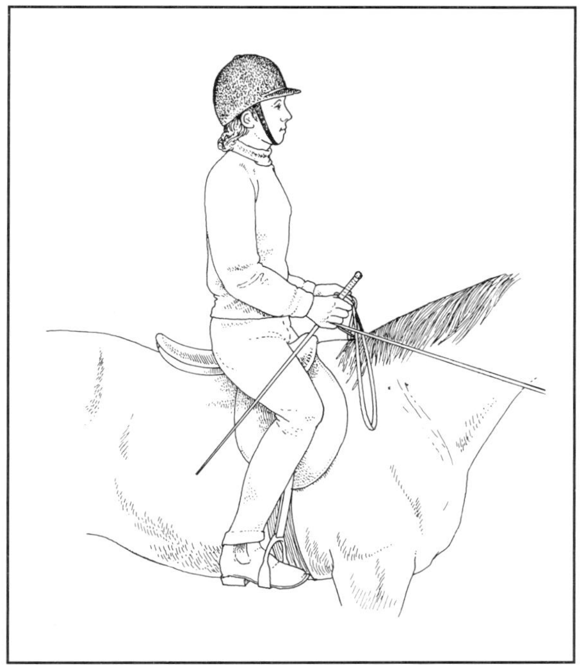

The correct way to carry a whip.

The whip used to reinforce a leg aid.

The whip This is brought into action only if the pony does not obey the leg aids. It should be used sharply once and your hand must be removed from the rein as you apply the whip to avoid confusing your pony. The whip should be applied just behind the leg that gave the aid.

A standard whip measures 74 cm (30 in) in length. When schooling a longer whip 91 cm (3 ft) may be used, without taking the hand from the rein.

Spurs Blunt spurs – that is, spurs without rowels – are the only acceptable type of spurs. They are worn with the necks pointing downwards and the arm of the spur parallel with the sole of the boot. The buckles always fasten on the outside of the boot. To use a spur correctly, you should turn your toe slightly outwards so that the side of the spur neck touches the pony's side. If you turn your foot out too far, the back of the spur will dig into the pony and this is incorrect. Spurs should only be worn by experienced riders.

A spur correctly fitted.

SCHOOLING

Schooling is the means by which rider and pony together achieve *harmony* and *balance*.

Flatwork This is the term given to schooling work performed in an arena, or manege. Flatwork covers work at the different paces, and changes of pace and direction. Circles and turns are used to encourage the pony to bend his body correctly. It helps to build up the rider's feel for the horse, so that she learns to know without having to ask a spectator whether her mount's outline and pace are right.

A common fault among inexperienced riders, for example, is that they do not know, without looking down, whether the pony is leading with the correct leg at the canter. You should be able to feel which shoulder is slightly ahead of the other and which hind leg reaches the ground first.

Hillwork The best way of improving a pony's balance is to ride up and down hills.

The slope of the ground encourages him to get his weight off the forehand and builds up the muscles in his quarters. He also learns to use his hocks actively. In addition, this type of work is an excellent preliminary to jumping.

Effective schooling requires an understanding of the correct use of the aids.

USE OF THE AIDS

For the walk

When you ask a pony to move forward from a halt into a walk, you do so with your lower legs: a quick application of pressure on the pony's sides, followed by the give and take of your hands to correspond with the movements of the pony's head. When the walk is proceeding at a calm yet active pace, the hind leg should reach the ground in front of the print left by the foreleg on the same side. Occasionally, let the pony walk on a loose rein (which is how you should leave a dressage arena after you have completed a test). Allow the reins to slip through your fingers so that they become completely slack, while the pony stretches his head and neck.

The rider's position at the walk.

For the trot

Similar but slightly stronger aids are used to urge your pony into a trot, either from a halt or from a walk. Your legs and seat create impulsion, while your hands give sufficiently so as not to restrict the forward movement. You start to rise as the pony settles into the rhythm of the pace.

From time to time, change the diagonal. At the trot you rise when one diagonal pair of legs touches the ground and sit down on the other. If you sit for two beats, you change the diagonal that you rise on. It is more comfortable for your pony if you do this every so often.

An extended trot.

It is also a good idea to carry out a few movements at the sitting trot, consciously pushing your seat bones well into the saddle and trying not to bump. However, never continue at a sitting trot for too long as it can be very tiring.

For the canter

Prepare for the canter a few strides in advance of asking your pony to change his pace, and always see that the preceding pace is moving ahead with plenty of balance and impulsion. Sit down to the trot and indicate the direction of the canter by feeling the pony's mouth with the inside hand. Keep your inside leg on the pony's girth, but move your outside leg back a little so that you can apply pressure

Opposite Exercises done while the pony is going out at the walk, such as bending down to touch the toes, will improve the rider's balance and suppleness.

strongly and definitely to the pony's side behind the girth. If you have given the aids correctly and the pony responds properly, he should strike off into a true canter with his inside legs leading.

Many ponies favour one side more than the other. That is to say, if asked to canter in a straight line, they will always lead off with either the near side or off side legs. If you ride your pony in a circle with his favoured side

The transition from trot to canter, working on a curve. The pony collects himself to lead off with the correct – i.e., the inside – leg.

When a pony leads on the wrong – outside – leg at the canter, he is unbalanced. The rider should bring him back to the trot and give the correct aids.

on the inside, you will have no problems getting him to lead off correctly. Trouble arises when you ride round on the other rein (that is, in the other direction). To be in balance, he must lead with the other legs, which he may not want to do.

A pony which canters a circle with the outside legs leading is said to be cantering false or counter-leading. Sometimes, perhaps because you have given the wrong aids or he has misunderstood them, the pony will canter disunited. This means that his leading hind leg is on the opposite side to his leading foreleg.

If the strike-off is wrong, it must be corrected immediately by bringing the pony back to a trot and moving into a canter again. Flying changes, when a pony changes the leading legs without going out of a canter, should not be attempted until you and the pony are very experienced. Nevertheless, many ponies, especially those with natural balance and impulsion, will change legs instinctively to match changes of direction. You have only to watch a skilful little gymkhana pony as he nips in and out of bending poles to see this.

For the gallop
Use the aid for increased impulsion and take up the galloping position, with your weight forward on your knees and stirrups and your seat just out of the saddle. Shorten the reins slightly to maintain contact with the mouth.

For decreases in pace
Use quickly-applied pressure of the outside hand to slow the pony down, while your legs continue to supply impulsion. Make certain that the pony remains balanced and on the bit.

For the halt
The aids here are the same as for decreases in pace. It is important that your legs should stay in contact with the pony's sides as he stops, to avoid loss of impulsion and to

Top right A smooth halt with pony and rider nicely balanced.

Reining back. **Above right** The correct way. **Right** The wrong way.

prevent the tendency for him to step back. The halt should be square and straight, with the pony's weight spread evenly over his four legs.

For the rein back

It is quite difficult for a pony to walk backwards correctly without loss of balance. If his head goes up and his back hollows, he is unbalanced and resistant, and more schooling is needed in the forward paces. The aids for the rein back may seem contradictory to the pony because the rider's legs ask him to go forward while the hands hold him back. Lessons in the rein back should always be carried out quietly. You should never try to make him walk back too far – one step or two is sufficient at the beginning. As soon as he has stepped back the required number of strides, ask him to go forward again immediately, using the correct leg aid and giving with your hands.

JUMPING

The object of the rider when going over a jump is to give the pony as much help as possible by keeping the weight in the correct position at each phase. At the same time, you should relax and concentrate on maintaining good balance, impulsion and rhythm.

Allow the pony to choose the moment of take-off until you have learnt to judge it accurately yourself. Aim at going with him, and interfere as little as possible.

There are five phases to the jump, whether you are tackling knock-down fences in the show-ring or fixed fences on a cross-country course.

Phase one is the *approach*. The pony must be going forward with balance, impulsion and rhythm. Phase two is the *take-off*. As the pony approaches the jump, he lowers his head and stretches his neck, gathering himself for the moment of take-off. Energy for the spring comes from his hocks and his whole body foreshortens: his head comes up, his neck shortens and he lifts himself off the ground, folding his forelegs under him. Phase three is the *moment of suspension*. This is the moment when he is in mid-air. His legs are tucked up under him, his head and neck stretch forwards and downwards to their fullest extent. His back should be rounded, forming a 'bascule'. Phase four is the *landing*. As the pony approaches the ground, he braces his forelegs and raises his head and neck to keep his balance and to be ready to move away as soon as his hind legs hit the ground. The final phase is the *recovery*. This is the first stride after landing, and the start of the approach to the next jump. His hocks should be well under him in order to regain balance, impulsion and rhythm.

The rider's position

You must make certain that your weight is over the pony's centre of gravity at the take-off and during the moment of suspension, returning to the upright position on landing. This is done by bending forward at the hips – not the waist. It is easier to support this movement if your stirrup-leathers are shortened, making the angles formed by the knee and ankle joints more acute. You should be able to take and hold the jumping position at both the trot and the canter, showing that you have a balanced, independent seat, and that you do not have to hang on to the reins or rest your hands on the pony's neck in order to maintain it. You must be able to give with the

The five phases of the jump. **From left**: the approach; the take-off; the moment of suspension; the landing; and the recovery.

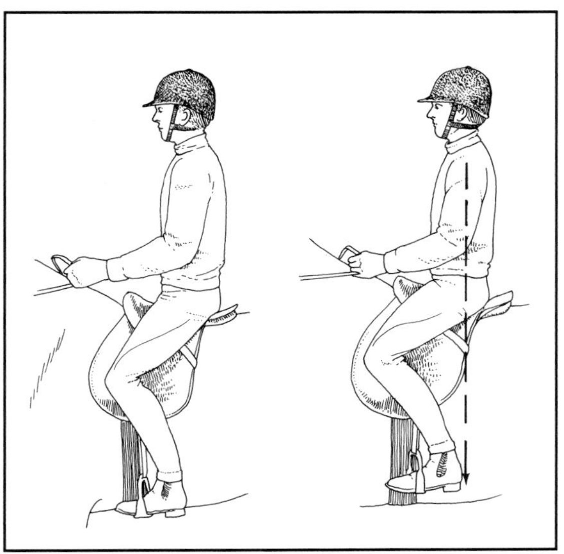

Stirrup-leathers should be shortened for jumping. **Left** The length for riding on the flat. **Right** Jumping length.

The jumping position. The rider is balanced, without resting on the hands.

hands, following the movement of the pony's head and neck, while you are jumping.

At the approach You should sit lightly in the saddle without interfering with the pony's balance and impulsion. Your lower legs rest against the pony's side and your hands keep a gentle but steady contact with the pony's mouth.

At take-off and moment of suspension Fold forward at the hips, keeping your back flat and your head up, looking ahead. Never be tempted to look down at the jump, or lean to one side, or your weight will be unevenly distributed and the pony will have a harder job to keep his rhythm. Your heels should be well down, joints supple, and your lower leg should not slip back. Your hands continue to keep a light contact with the pony's mouth and to give with the movement of head and neck.

At landing and recovery Your body moves back into the upright position, and your leg lightly touches the pony's side ready to get him into his stride for the next approach, while your eyes look towards the next jump.

Points to remember

* Practise the fold forward from the hips at trot and canter.
* Beware of throwing your hands up the pony's neck, so that contact between your fingers and the pony's mouth is lost. This is a common fault with beginners, often caused by fear of being left behind, and it produces inadvertent jabbing at the pony's mouth. The sudden loss of contact may confuse the pony and eventually lead to his refusing.
* Consciously keep your lower leg in the right position, with the heels down.
* Never fiddle with the reins or flap your legs wildly.
* Keep your shoulders soft and flexible.
* Keep your back straight.
* Keep your head up and look straight in front of you.

Schooling over trotting poles

Trotting poles are beneficial schooling aids to both pony and rider. This type of schooling helps a pony to learn obedience and to develop balance, rhythm and co-ordination. It also encourages him to lower his head and neck, to round his back and engage his hocks. It helps the rider to develop balance, rhythm and timing, and teaches her how to judge distance and placing.

Jumping poles may be used as trotting poles. They are set parallel to each other on

Trotting poles should be used to improve the pony's balance.

the ground, between 1.2 and 1.5 m (4 and 5 ft) apart, depending on the size of the pony. A minimum of three poles should be used, and they should be pegged to the ground to prevent them from rolling about.

Always take trotting poles at a rising trot. If possible, ask someone else to watch whether each footfall is exactly in the centre of the space between the poles. It is very important that the rider should not look down. You must look up and forwards, otherwise the pony could become unbalanced.

When your pony is working confidently and correctly over trotting poles, you can introduce a small schooling fence some 2.7 m (9 ft) away from the last pole.

TYPES OF FENCE

There are four types of fence; they are described according to their shape. Different shapes present different degrees of difficulty.

The easiest type is the *sloping or ascending fence*, of which the triple bar is the best example. The lowest element consists of a pole at or near ground level at the front of the fence. The rest of the fence ascends away from the direction of approach. The next fence in the difficulty rating is the *pyramid* (tiger trap or double oxer), in which the middle section is the highest part. Then comes the *upright* (post and rails, gate), sometimes called a *vertical*. To judge the take-off point correctly for this type of fence, remember that the distance between the take-off point and the base of the fence should be about equal to the height of the fence. The most difficult fence to jump is the *true parallel* (parallel bars or planks with a pole behind). Both parts of the parallel should be of the same height.

BUILDING JUMPS

Ready-made show-jumps are expensive to buy. Young riders have been known to mortgage their birthday and Christmas presents for years to come in exchange for a set of six professionally built fences, but not everyone has even that opportunity. Most people make do with what they can find around home, and there is no end to the ingenuity that goes into the making of a home-made jumping course.

If there is any money available for jumps, it is best to spend it on proper poles. Jumping stands and wings can be devised and built out of a variety of materials, but poles need to be fairly heavy and substantial to be safe to use.

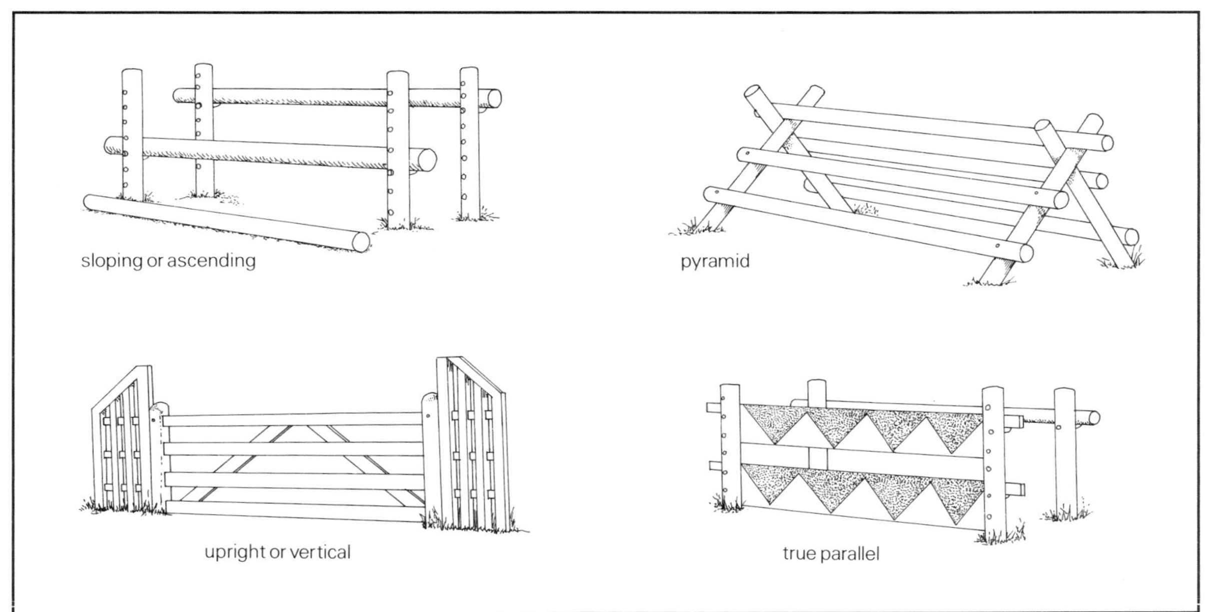

Examples of the four different types of fence.

They should, for example, be not less than 10 cm (4 in) in diameter and at least 3 m (10 ft) long, and even unpainted poles of this description are expensive to buy.

To be able to build a reasonable jumping course, you will need at least four jumps, of which one or two should be spreads. This adds up to at least six pairs of jump stands and a few fillers to supplement the poles.

Making your own jumps

If you are good with your hands and can do some carpentry – or know someone who can – it is worth buying wood from a timber yard and making jump stands that match the professional ones. You will need metal cups to fit your home-made stands, but your jumps will look good and should last. If you are hopeless at carpentry, there is no need to despair; many other things can be used to make jumps.

Oil drums Large oil drums can be used in two ways. Standing on end, with blocks fitted to them to support poles, they make sturdy jump stands. Laid on their sides, they make a substantial filler. If you use them on their sides, bang wooden pegs into the ground on each side so that the drums cannot roll. You can paint the drums bright colours.

To make the most of a small number of oil drums, cut them in half and fix each half to an upright post to create stable jump stands. The advantage of using only half an oil drum is that the stands are reasonably light to move about.

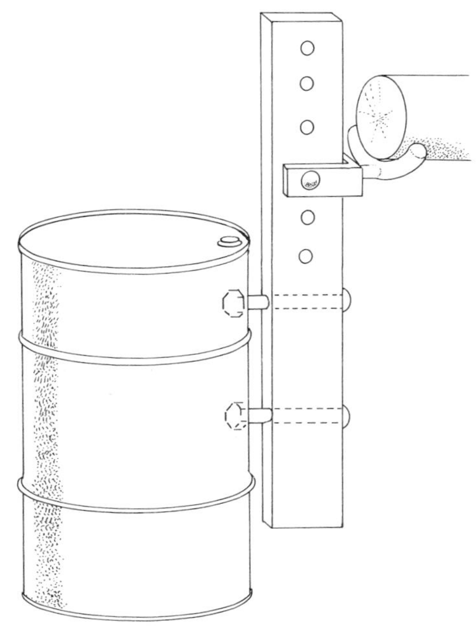

A large oil drum used as jump stand.

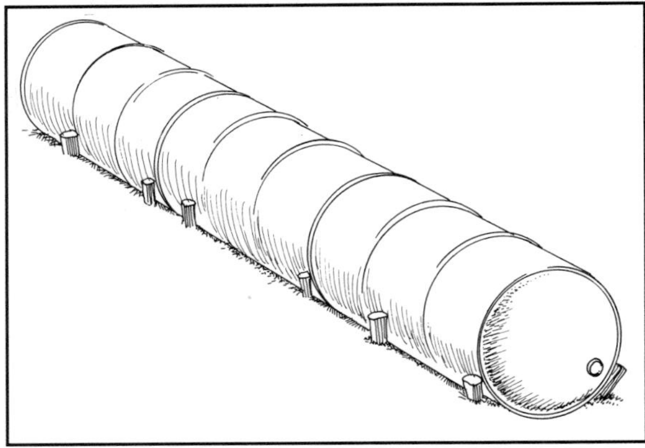

Oil drums laid on their sides and pegged to prevent them from rolling, make an inviting fence.

Old oil drums can often be obtained from factories which have no further use for them once the contents are finished. If you approach the manager or foreman, you may be able to buy the drums very cheaply. Try to get ones which are not rusty, and paint them with a metal primer as soon as you get them home. Always use a non-toxic paint, especially if the jumps are to stay in the same field as your pony, just in case he takes it into his head to lick the paint.

Plastic chemical containers These containers come in various sizes, having been used to hold fertilizers or swimming-pool chemicals.

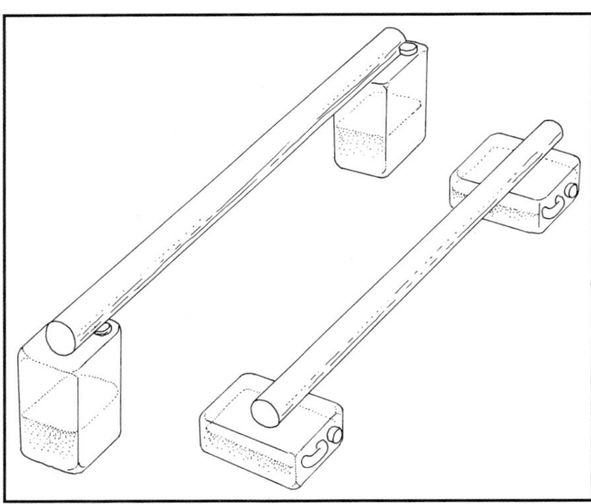

Plastic containers filled with water provide a stable base for a jump. They can be used either upright or on their sides, to vary the height of the poles.

Farmers or owners of large swimming-pools may be willing to sell them to you at a low price. Like the drums, they can be painted in bright colours, but you should always rinse them thoroughly before use. If you half-fill them with water, they will stand upright.

The containers can be used to support poles at different heights, depending on whether they are on their sides or not. A row of them makes a good filler.

Wooden pallets

Many industrial sites and factories have old pallets which they no longer need. A polite word with the foreman will often allow you to pick over the ones they have discarded and intend to burn, and you will be able to take away as many as you need. You can cut them in half horizontally and use them as a framework for a brush filler, stuffing the middle with brushwood and trimming the tops.

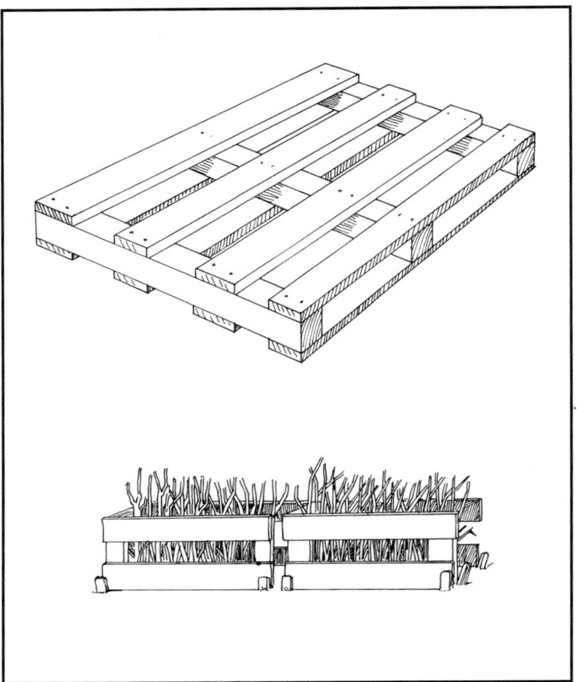

An old pallet, cut in half and filled with brushwood, can be turned into an effective brush fence.

Alternatively, face them with plywood or hardboard and paint them to resemble a wall. It may be necessary to fit supports to the bases to make them stand upright.

Pole-cups

These are expensive to buy, and you will need a large number if you are to give your

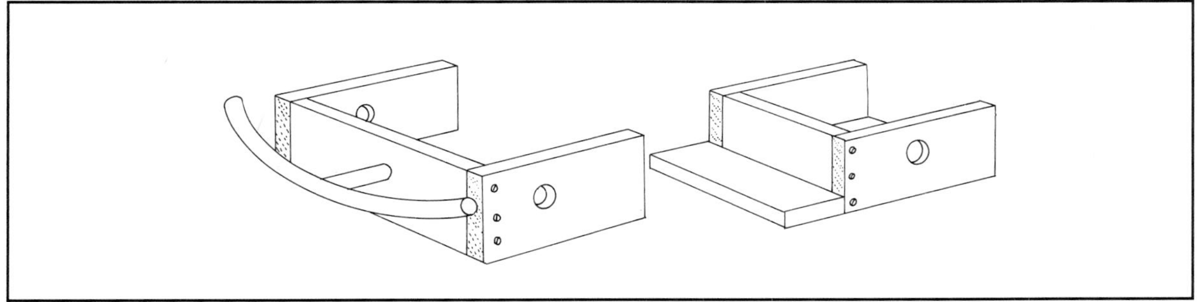

Home-made pole-cups, using wood offcuts or pieces of metal.

jumping course plenty of variety. You can, however, make quite adequate pole-cups out of wooden off-cuts (obtainable cheaply at most timber yards).

Old tyres

An inviting schooling fence can be made with old tyres, matched as far as possible for size and thickness. Thread them on to a pole and hang the pole on two stands so that the bottom of the tyres is just resting on the ground. Tyre replacement centres may let you have a number of tyres for nothing if you explain why you want them.

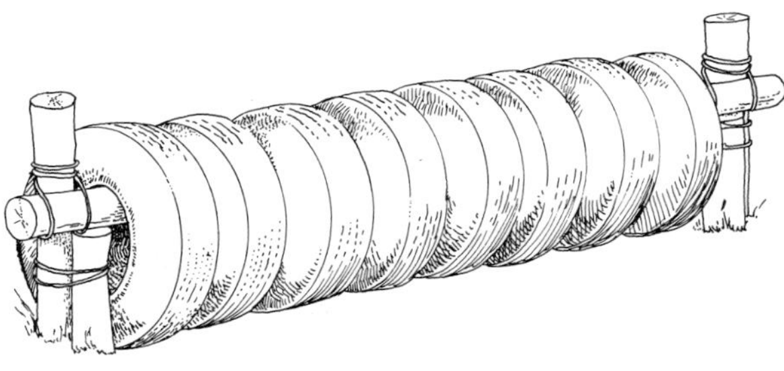

A jump made from old tyres threaded on to a pole.

Construction of a jumping course

The simplest layout for a jumping course is a figure of eight. Some jumps can be taken from either direction, but you should never try to jump a fence that slopes towards you because the pony can easily get too close at take-off.

All fences should have a good, easily visible ground line because a pony judges his point of take-off from the lowest part of the fence. Always remove spare pole-cups from jump stands. If a pony jumps crookedly, he could catch a leg on a projecting cup.

Fences should look solid, rather than airy. Fillers, even if only a row of oilcans, are used for this reason. When you raise the height of a post and rail fence, always add an extra pole

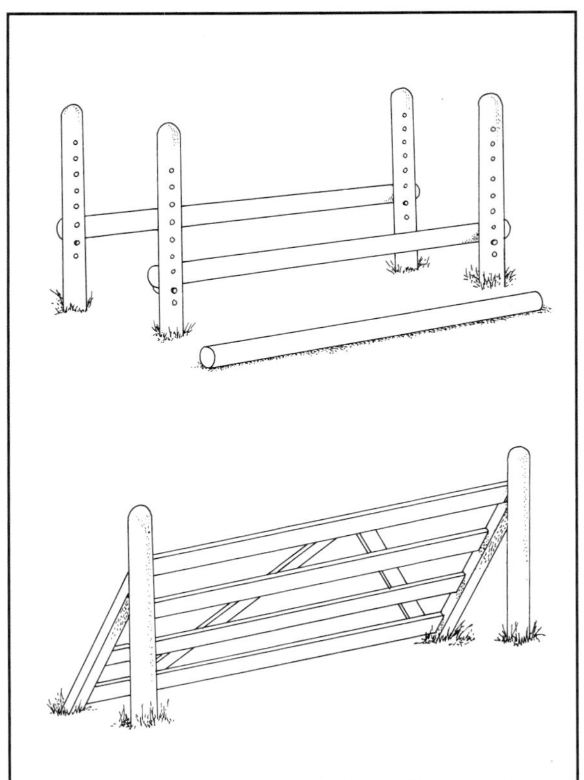

Ground lines are necessary to enable the pony to judge his point of take-off. **Top** A true ground line. **Bottom** A false ground line. It is dangerous to attempt a jump that slopes towards you as the pony cannot judge his take-off correctly and will probably get too close.

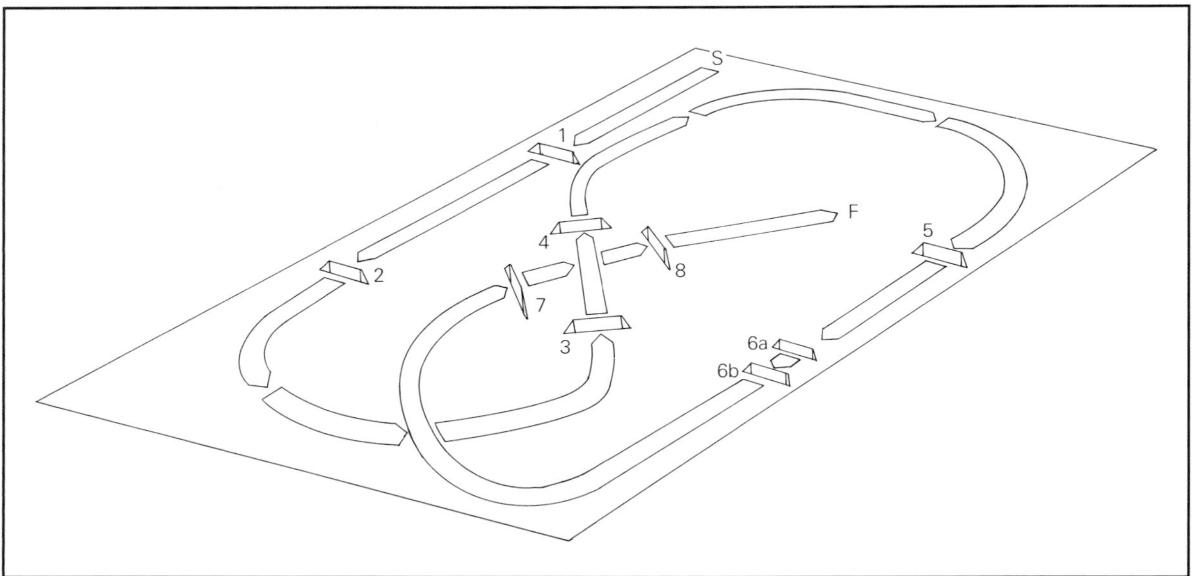

A simple figure-of-eight jumping course, using eight fences.

Number of non-jumping strides	PONY Trot	PONY Canter	HORSE Trot	HORSE Canter
Two	9.1 m (30 ft)	9.4–10.3 m (31–34 ft)	9.1–9.7 m (30–32 ft)	10.3–10.9 m (34–36 ft)
One	4.8–5.4 m (16–18 ft)	6.4–7.3 m (21–24 ft)	5.4 m (18 ft)	7.3–8.0 m (24–26½ ft)
None (Bounce)	2.7–3.0 m (9–10 ft)	3.0–3.6 m (10–12 ft)	2.7–3.3 m (9–11 ft)	3.3–4.2 m (11–14 ft)

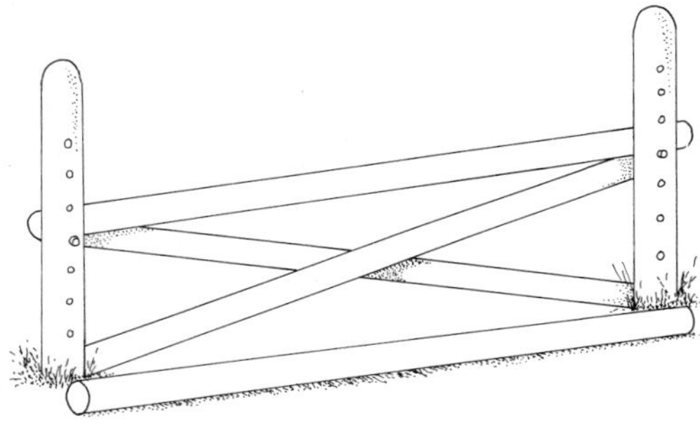

When raising the height of a fence, add two crossed poles to fill in the gap under the top pole, so that the jump is not too airy.

or use crossed poles under the top pole, to give a more solid appearance.

Never use a plank on the further side of a parallel fence.

Combinations are easier to take if the first element is an ascending jump. When building a double, it is important that the two elements are the correct distance apart; the table above gives an approximate guide. The distance varies according to the number of strides you decide to have between the two elements and the pace at which the fence will be approached. If the fence is to be approached at the trot, the distance is shorter than if it is to be approached at the canter.

When building a double for a novice pony, make certain that there are two non-jumping strides between the two elements. Doubles with one non-jumping stride and 'bounce' fences (that is, with no non-jumping stride) should not be used until a pony is experienced at jumping.

CHAPTER 8
Shows and gymkhanas

Once you have a pony of your own, you will almost certainly want to take him to shows and gymkhanas. Competitions are fun and it is exciting to win rosettes to pin up on your bedroom wall.

HOW TO ENTER

The gymkhana season begins in the spring, and continues to the autumn. Apart from shows and gymkhanas, there are also hunter trials and one-day events, but if you are a beginner you should start off with small, local gymkhanas where the emphasis is very much on fun.

These events are usually advertised in the local papers or by means of posters put up in the area. Almost all advertisements will invite you to send a stamped addressed envelope (s.a.e.) for details to the secretary, who in due course will send you back a schedule. Because of the cost, most organizers nowadays produce a duplicated schedule, which can be quite bulky, so be sensible and send an envelope that measures at least 23 × 10 cm (9 × 4 in).

Once the schedule arrives, make a note of the closing date for entries, and then work out which events you would like to have a go at. Be sure to get your entries to the secretary in time: late entries may not be accepted at all, and if they are accepted they usually cost extra.

Even beginners can usually find quite a variety of classes for which they are eligible. Gymkhana events are divided into age groups; jumping classes may include a minimus jumping, plus novice events for ponies of different heights. There will probably be clear round jumping, a handy pony class, and often one or other of the two jumping events which are regarded as gymkhana classes: Chase-me-Charlie and barrel elimination.

If you are eight years old or under and not absolutely confident that you can control your pony in a competition, you would probably be wise to enter the leading-rein gymkhana events, in which all competitors have to be led.

Most gymkhana events consist of the standard – and most popular – games. These include: bending, where you have to weave up and down a line of poles; potato or old sock races, where you have to collect potatoes or socks in turn and drop them in a bucket; flag races, in which you transfer coloured flags from one cone to another; and musical elimination games, such as musical mats or musical wands. Races which require little equipment are also popular with organizers – these include walking and trotting races, where you will be penalized if you go faster than the pace allowed, or run-and-lead, where you have to dismount from your pony half-way through the race and lead him to the finish.

Many of these games are included in the list for leading-rein competitors.

Chase-me-Charlie is a jumping event in which all competitors follow one another over one or two show jumps. The jumps start very low but are gradually raised as each competitor attempts them. Anyone who knocks down a jump or refuses is out. Eventually, the last survivors may be tackling jumps which are quite high, although, of course, any competitor may withdraw from the

Gymkhana games in action. **Above** Leaning low to ensure that the potato goes in the bucket. **Below** A bending race.

Above A mad dash to the centre in musical mats. **Below** A flag is whipped out of the cone during the flag race.

class if she thinks the jump has reached too great a height for herself or her pony to tackle.

In barrel elimination, competitors again follow one another over a jump, but this one consists of a row of oil drums. Gradually, the oil drums are removed until only one is left, and the winner is the pony which jumps it cleanly, without rapping it or side-stepping.

Some shows expect advance entries for jumping and showing classes but invite competitors to make entries for gymkhana events on the day. This means exactly what it says; you do not make any entries or send any entry fees for gymkhana events until you arrive at the show-ground. Clear round jumping is always entered on the day. This is not a competition in the sense that it produces winners, but it is a good way for someone who does not own any show jumps to try her pony out over a proper show-jumping course. You pay the entry fee to the steward in the collecting ring, ride round the course and collect a rosette if you finish the round without any penalties. You can have as many goes as you like as long as you pay the entry fee each time. The height of the course may be raised as the day progresses.

Handy pony competitions require entrants to complete a course of hazards, which may or may not include one or two jumps. You will probably have to transfer a sack or basket from one place to another, open and shut a gate, carry a bucket, hang out washing, lead your pony over a set of cavaletti, perhaps ride part of the course bareback; in fact, anything that the ingenuity of the organizers can devise. The course will be timed, penalties such as knocking down a jump will take the form of seconds added, and the winner is the one who completes the hazards in the fastest time. A handy pony competition is a good contest for sturdy, unflappable ponies which take everything in their stride but are not brilliant jumpers or very nippy gymkhana participants.

WHAT TO DO ON ARRIVAL

When you enter a show for the first time you may be worried about what you actually have to do as soon as you arrive on the show-ground.

The first point to remember is that you should arrive early. If it is a local show, within hacking distance, try to set off early enough to arrive at least half an hour before your first event. Your journey should be taken at an easy pace, so that your pony is not hot and tired before you get there and has plenty of energy for the forthcoming events. Take a headcollar with you, either strapped round your waist or on the pony under the bridle, and find a shady spot as soon as you arrive where you can tie up your pony. Unless your parents are following later in the car, you will have to take your picnic lunch and items from your grooming kit, such as a body brush and hoof-pick, in a satchel.

Collect your competitor's number from the secretary's tent or caravan. The number is printed on thin cardboard and has a piece of plastic string long enough to tie round your waist. Position it so that the number is displayed in the small of your back. You may be issued with a ticket for each event you enter and you have to give up the ticket to the steward when you go into the ring.

Check whether the show is running to time, especially if you have arrived after the show has started and your events are not due to begin until later in the day. It is not unusual for classes to start anything up to an hour or so late. If there is more than one arena or ring, find out which ring your events are in and where it is situated on the field. After that you can relax, find your friends and watch other competitors in action.

Your pony may well benefit from a period of warming up. Try to find a reasonably empty corner of the show-ground and put him quietly through his paces. There is usually a practice jump near the jumping arenas, but this is not an invitation to spend all day jumping. You should at all times think about your pony's welfare; never, for example, use him as a grandstand or gallop about the field to show everyone how fast he can go. The time for going fast is in the ring, not out of it.

Listen to loudspeaker announcements. Competitors for each event are usually called to the appropriate collecting ring about ten minutes before the event is due to begin. When you hear your class announced, make your way to the collecting point, but do not enter the arena until you are told to do so by the steward in charge.

Most gymkhana events are run in heats, with a final of six. Organizers have different methods of arranging the heats. Some leave it to the competitors, which means that all the good ones, who are well aware of the quality of the opposition, will try to avoid being in one heat together. Some heats are drawn, with competitors taking coloured counters out of a bag, so that all those with the same colour are put in the same heat.

Once you are in the ring for your heat, the judge or ring steward will briefly explain the rules. Do listen carefully at this stage; if you are disqualified later for contravening the rules, it is no use complaining that you didn't know or that this wasn't the rule that operated at the last show. Every judge is at liberty to alter the rules if she wishes and you must abide by the ones in force at that moment. If necessary, ask how many will be kept from each heat for the final; there is no point in tiring your pony unnecessarily by riding flat out to win if you are going to qualify anyway by coming second. Finalists are usually asked to wait in a corner until all the heats have finished. If you are lucky or skilled enough to make the final, jump off your pony, cross the stirrups over the saddle and rest your pony's back while you are waiting.

Finally, never complain at the judge's decision, even if you think you have been unfairly treated. The judges do their best to arbitrate fairly; maybe you did indeed beat the girl on the skewbald by a nose, but remember that next time there is a doubtful decision it might benefit you. At all shows you go to, it is possible to lodge an objection, but you will have to accompany it with a money deposit which will be forefeited if your objection is overruled. The only grounds on which you should object to another competitor is where you *know* the conditions of entry have been violated and can prove it–for example, if the rider is over age or the pony is over height.

Jumping classes, including minimus jumping (that is, for ponies of say 13.2 hh and under and riders aged 12 years and under), are normally run under standard rules. Each knock down counts four faults, the first refusal or run-out is three faults, the second six and the third, even if they are not all at the same jump, is elimination. If you take the wrong course or leave the arena before the round is finished (not unusual in novice classes where the pony can be wilful and the rider not firm enough) you will be eliminated.

Competitors with clear rounds, or equality of faults for first place, are invited to take part in a jump-off. This may be over the same course against the clock, over a raised course against the clock, or over a shortened and raised course against the clock. However it is organized, the jump-off is usually timed, and the pony with the lowest number of faults and the fastest round is the winner.

At the end of the day, hopefully with a number of rosettes and a pleasant sense of well-being, you have to ride home. Remember that your pony is tired, even though you may be feeling elated, and you should ride him home carefully and quietly. If necessary, get off and walk part of the way.

When you get home, remove the saddle and rub off the saddle marks, then turn him out into his field. He is better off being turned out straightaway than being put in a stable. Once in his familiar field, he can roll, have a drink and relax. Later on, after an hour or so, take him a feed.

The next day, catch him up and check him over for signs of stiffness. If you ride him, and there is no reason why you shouldn't, take him gently, just enough to work any stiffness out of him.

When you begin to go to shows and gymkhanas, you will no doubt stick to the local ones which are within easy hacking distance. However, in due course you will want to go to shows further afield and will need some form of transport to get there. By then, you will probably be ready for the next stage in your riding career, the acquisition of a second, competition, pony.

Pages 82–83 Vaulting on at speed may mean the difference between winning and losing. The sequence of actions starts with the first spring. Note the shortness of the rider's reins, so that her left hand is controlling the direction of the pony, while her right hand grasps the offside of the saddle flap helping the upward movement of her jump. The forward speed of the pony helps the rider to swing her right leg over the back of the saddle. By the end, she is already in the saddle, and her balance should be good enough for her not to need her feet in the stirrup-irons.

1

2

3

4

5

6

CHAPTER 9

The pony's health

Ponies are tough little creatures and, by and large, manage to remain remarkably healthy. As long as you follow the general rules of pony care, there is no reason why your pony should not lead a long and trouble-free life. And one of the first rules is to try to prevent illnesses before they arise.

INOCULATION

Horses can be given protection against tetanus and equine influenza with a single, annual injection.

Tetanus (also known as lockjaw) is an unpleasant, often fatal disease of the central nervous system, and it is very important that your pony is inoculated against it. It is caused by a germ which is found in the horse's intestines, in its dung, and often in the soil. In these places, it is harmless, but should it get into a suitable breeding site, such as a deep cut, it can breed and multiply. Puncture wounds, which are often hard to spot, are the most likely areas of infection. They provide the sort of airless conditions in which the tetanus germ flourishes. The incubation period for tetanus can be quite lengthy and an unprotected pony can develop tetanus long after the wound which caused the disease has cleared up.

The symptoms of tetanus are an inability to open the mouth (hence the alternative name, lockjaw), a tendency to shy at sudden sounds, head-jerking if the pony is flicked under the jaw, and the appearance in the eye of the third eyelid (or haw). Gradually, the pony finds it more and more difficult to move and his body becomes rigid, with forelegs and hind legs extended.

Luckily, inoculation is highly effective. After an initial dose and booster, the annual injection gives total immunity. As long as your pony's protection is kept up to date, there is no danger that the animal will become infected through a tiny, unnoticed cut.

Tetanus can also affect human beings, and it is one of the diseases which the ordinary routine injections guard against. Because you are going to spend much of your time around horses, however, it is sensible to visit your doctor and ask for a booster injection to be given to you.

The pony's anti-tetanus jab may be given alone or combined with an inoculation against equine influenza. The flu jab, in some people's eyes, is essential. Others believe that it does more harm than good. However, equine flu, while not fatal, is very infectious and can keep a pony off work for several weeks. The symptoms are fever and coughing, and the treatment is isolation, rest and a light diet.

If your pony is kept at livery, the stable-owner may insist on the inoculation, on the grounds that as the infection can spread quickly through the stables and prevent other horses from taking part in competitions it is better to provide whatever protection is available. Some places, such as racecourses and agricultural show-grounds, will not allow any horse to enter the premises without a valid vaccination certificate.

The initial two doses must be given between three weeks and three months apart, and these are followed by annual booster injections. After each injection the pony has to be rested for about a week, so you will have to plan the inoculation timetable to avoid any special events in which you could be hoping to take part. Most ponies show little reaction to the injection, although a few may seem lethargic for two or three weeks.

WORMING

Worming is another essential part of preventative medicine. All horses have parasites in their stomach and intestines. If they are there in very small quantities, the effect on the pony will be barely noticeable. Danger arises when the parasite count builds up.

Of the three types of worms found in horses, red worms (strongyles) are the most dangerous. A badly infested pony loses condition rapidly, looks thin and has a staring coat. He may suffer from anaemia and bouts of colic. Round worms are quite commonly found in horses, and tapeworms are occasionally present.

The parasites form a continuous cycle. Worm eggs are passed out of the pony in his droppings. As the pony grazes, he picks up the larvae and swallows them. They hatch out in his stomach and live on the food which should be nourishing the pony.

A field which is continuously grazed by horses can become severely infected with parasites, and these can affect all the ponies which live in it. The first line of attack is to care for the field properly. This means using any of the remedies which will break the worm cycle: picking up droppings regularly, cutting and harrowing, resting the field, or grazing sheep or cattle in it for a time.

The second is to worm the pony. Worm powders and pastes can be bought from the vet, who will advise you on the best sort to buy and the amount you will need for the size of your pony.

Powders are easily administered as they are tasteless and can be mixed with the pony's feed. Pastes come in throwaway syringes. The syringe is inserted into the corner of the pony's mouth and the paste squirted on to his tongue. Most ponies should be wormed every eight to ten weeks.

Bot-flies can also be treated with a worming paste or powder. The bot-fly lays its eggs on the pony's coat, usually down the legs and on the shoulders and flanks. They are noticeable in late summer, especially on a dark-coloured pony, showing up as dozens of little yellow specks. No amount of brushing will remove them, although they can be painstakingly picked off with the finger-nails or a safety razor.

As the eggs start hatching, they seem to cause irritation, making the pony lick or nibble at his legs. As he does this, he swallows the grubs and they attach themselves to the stomach wall. They stay there for several months, interfering with the pony's digestion, until eventually, the following spring, they pass out of the pony in his droppings.

Anti-bot-fly granules or paste can be given to the pony in the late autumn. These kill the grubs while they are in the stomach. It may be difficult, however, to get your pony to accept the granules, even when they are mixed thoroughly with his feed, and the paste and syringe method of application may be the only effective one to use.

PROBLEMS WHICH CAN AFFECT A PONY AT GRASS

Spring is the time to be especially vigilant in the care of your pony, as there are various problems which can crop up.

Lice

Lice increase rapidly as the weather gets warmer. These little, wingless insects collect in the hair roots of the mane and tail and cause intense irritation as they hatch. The pony rubs the affected parts against fence posts and tree trunks in an effort to relieve the itching and often rubs away portions of the mane and tail as well.

If you suspect an outbreak of lice, inspect the mane and tail area thoroughly and take advice if you are not absolutely sure what you are looking for. Lice can sometimes be mistaken for scurf. Treatment is by means of louse powder, or the use of a wash or spray. The powder should be worked well into the hair with the fingers. Only the hatched lice will be killed, however, and you should repeat the treatment ten days or a fortnight later to catch any new hatchings.

Laminitis

This is another common problem with grass-fed ponies. Its basic cause is overfeeding and under-exercise, and is most likely to occur in the spring when a pony gorges himself to bursting on the new grass. Laminitis is sometimes called fever of the foot or founder. It gets its name from the laminae, layers of tissue which separate the pedal bone from the wall of the hoof. These become greatly inflamed and the effect on the pony is like having to force a badly swollen foot into a very tight shoe. Not surprisingly, a pony with laminitis is extremely reluctant to move.

The first sign of laminitis is when the pony, while standing in the field, pushes his forelegs far forward so that his weight is taken on the heels. He may rest the front feet in turn. Laminitis always starts in the front feet but it can spread to the back ones as well. A pony with the disease in all four feet will throw all his weight back on to the heels. The outer wall of each affected hoof will feel hot.

It is essential to get the pony back to a stable, but this is easier said than done and will certainly take a long time. Some relief from the pain can be gained by cooling the feet with water, either by trickling water from a hose on to the hooves, or by standing the pony in a stream of running water. As a last resort, you could try placing each foot in turn in a bowl of cold water.

You should call the vet as soon as you have managed to get the pony into a stable. Modern drugs can help the condition by reducing the inflammation and easing the pain. Other remedies include removing the pony's shoes and encouraging him to walk about in order to improve the circulation. A vital ingredient in the recovery process is putting the pony on a very restricted diet.

It may be several weeks before the pony gets better and can move freely again without pain. Even then, the feet may be left with dropped soles and ridges of horn round the hoof. The blacksmith's help will be needed in getting the feet into good shape again.

When a pony has had laminitis once, he can easily get it again, and care must be taken to see that he never gets too fat nor has access to too much rich grass. In spring, this may mean bringing the pony into a stable and keeping him without food for hours at a time. Alternatively, he may be turned out into a paddock which is almost bare of grass.

Always remember, too, that laminitis can occur at any time of the year. Too much food of any sort, coupled with insufficient work to burn up the calories, can put the pony at risk.

Sweet itch

Sweet itch is a condition that occurs only during the summer. If you bought your pony during the winter months, you may not have realized that he is prone to it. Unfortunately, it is a chronic complaint and, although various forms of treatment exist and will no doubt be suggested by friends, there is no absolutely foolproof remedy.

Sweet itch is a skin complaint, believed to be caused by an allergic reaction to a particular type of biting insect. The effect is an acute irritation of the mane and tail area and around the face, causing the pony to rub himself against the nearest available tree or post until he produces sores. In the early evenings, when the insects are at their worst, he will trot round and round the field in a futile attempt to get away from the midges' attentions.

The most successful remedy is to stable the pony by day and turn him into his field after dark, but unless stable and field are close at hand, this is not always possible. Benzyl benzoate or sulphanilamide may be applied to the sores and various fly-repellents may give temporary protection. In very severe cases, the vet may suggest cortisone injections to try and overcome the allergy. Sweet itch starts around May or June and continues until the autumn.

Galls

Galls or sores sometimes occur with soft, grass-fed ponies and are caused by chafing, either by the saddle or by the girth. Salt-and-water solution (one dessert-spoon of salt to 57 cl (UK 1 pt; USA $2\frac{1}{2}$ cups) of water) can help to dry up the sores, but you should also look for the cause. If necessary, have the saddle re-stuffed or change the girth and wait until the galls are healed before using the saddle again. The salt-and-water solution will help to harden the skin.

Coughing

This is not necessarily a sign of illness but it always requires investigation. If a pony coughs once or twice at the start of a ride or when the weather is dry and dusty, he may simply be clearing a tickle from his throat. If the cough persists, especially if the pony has a runny nose, suspect some sort of infection and call the vet. Do not ride the pony.

Too much exertion when the pony has a cough can lead to the chronic condition known as broken wind. This means that some of the lung cavities have broken down; a cure is not possible although you can prevent the condition from getting worse. Essentially it means that he is only capable of light work; he must never be ridden hard, he must not be allowed to eat, even grass, for an hour before a ride, and his hay should be dampened before it is given to him. He needs plenty of fresh air and will do better living out than in a stable.

Broken wind is caused by riding a coughing pony before the cough has cleared up or by galloping unfit, grass-fed ponies.

A persistent cough with no other symptoms may be caused by lung worms. A laboratory test on the pony's dung will indicate the presence of lung worms and the vet will prescribe powders or paste to get rid of them. Ponies rarely pick up lung worms and if they do so it is almost certainly because they have come into contact with donkeys, which are common carriers of the parasite even when they themselves are unaffected.

Sweating

A grass-fed pony will sweat easily, especially if he has a thick winter coat. When you return from a ride, always give the pony time to cool down by walking the last half-mile (1km) home before you turn him out into the field. If you have to stand around in a chill wind with a sweating pony, walk him about quietly and cover his loins with a rug or coat.

The first thing a pony does when he is loose in his field is to get down on the ground and roll. This is perfectly normal and nothing to worry about even if he rolls more than once.

When a pony sweats for no obvious reason, he may be ill and you should look for other symptoms. Listlessness, trembling, dull eyes, loss of appetite are all signs that something is wrong, and you should call the vet. If a sweating pony keeps kicking or biting at his stomach, is restless and keeps getting down, rolling and getting up again, he is displaying all the signs of *colic*, which is indigestion. Colic can be caused by a number of things: overeating, eating poor quality food, drinking too much and too soon after a meal, exercising too soon after eating, or it may have a more serious cause.

Whatever the reason, professional help is essential. While you are waiting for the vet to arrive, try to keep the pony warm by covering him with rugs and, if necessary, holding a hot-water bottle to his belly. You should try to get him into a stable (if you have none of your own, most horse-owners will be willing to help a pony in distress) where he will have to stay until he recovers. If you can, keep him moving and try not to let him roll. He rolls to relieve the pain, but if he throws himself about too severely, he could twist a gut.

Fortunately, colic does not happen very often, particularly if you are vigilant in your care of the pony.

LAMENESS

Ponies can go lame for a variety of reasons, from a simple bruising of the sole to a severe sprain. Lameness is not easy to detect, especially if it is slight, but it will show up best at a trot. The pony should be trotted along a hard, level surface and watched from in front and behind. If the injury is in a foreleg, the pony will raise his head when the unsound leg hits the ground and nod downwards on the sound one. In a hind leg, the quarters on the sound side will droop more than the lame side.

Unless the cause of the lameness is obvious, such as a cut or swelling, look first at the hoof. Pick out the feet to satisfy yourself that the pony has not picked up a stone or nail, and tap the sole gently to check that there is no inflammation. A call to the vet is always a good precaution.

TEETHING PROBLEMS

The most common cause of eating difficulties lies with the teeth. A horse's teeth are constantly growing, but the rate of growth is usually matched by the rate of wear. Sometimes, however, and this is particularly prevalent in older ponies, the teeth do not wear down quickly enough and grow too long. You should always suspect this if your pony takes a long time over his food or drops bits out while he is eating, a practice known as quidding. Ask the vet to inspect the teeth and, if necessary, to rasp them down.

CHAPTER 10

Mainly for parents

From the moment you become a pony-owner to the time you have grown up, your parents will be your partners in the pony-owning venture. Even if they know nothing at all about horses at the outset, they will over the years become very knowledgeable, because there is no way in which they can avoid being involved. This section gives them some idea of what they are getting involved in.

At the beginning, a parent's involvement is principally financial. It is unrealistic to expect any child to be able to pay the costs of looking after a pony all by herself. Even if you own a field, the upkeep of a pony can run into several pounds a week.

The cost is not spread evenly throughout the year. In summer, when a pony is feeding almost solely on grass, he is cheap to keep. In winter, hay and concentrates soon run up big bills at the corn-chandlers. Shoeing expenses crop up every eight weeks or so, and veterinary bills – even for routine things like worming powders and anti-tetanus and anti-flu vaccinations – add to the annual cost.

You can be sure that, whatever a pony has – in the way of saddlery, grooming kits, clothing, and so on – his young owner will always think that he needs more. Anti-sweat rugs, summer sheets, tail bandages, leg bandages, travelling bandages, tail guards, rubber reins, drop nosebands, grooming kit boxes, buckets, haynets, fly fringes; the list never gets any shorter. Hoof-picks are forever getting lost and have to be replaced; saddles need re-stuffing from time to time; whips vanish into thin air.

The rider grows and needs new clothes: jodhpur boots fall apart, one pair of jodhpurs is superseded by two, three, even four or five pairs, a tweed jacket is joined by a showing jacket.

The Pony Club subscription comes up once a year. Show entry fees, which are quite small while the rider is still on the leading rein, get more expensive as pony and rider progress to bigger and better competitions.

Competitions, in turn, lead to even more expense. The velvet-covered riding hat is fine for gymkhanas, but once a child starts entering Pony Club events, she will need a proper crash hat, and for cross-country riding a back protector and a rugby shirt in her chosen colours.

INSURANCE

A pony is a valuable animal; it is also a living creature subject to illness and accidents, sometimes fatal. It should be regarded as an investment, and protected as such.

There are a number of insurance policies on the market, advertised in the horse magazines. All that is necessary is to choose the most suitable, fill in the proposal form on the advertisement, enclose a cheque for the premium, and post it off. Alternatively, insurance can be arranged through a broker.

Policies are usually graded to cater for different needs. Basic insurance will provide cover against loss or injury incurred during ordinary hacking and Pony Club events. Some activities, such as hunting, attract higher premiums. There are clauses covering veterinary fees, permanent disablement of the animal, and theft of the pony. Saddlery can be covered. And a trailer can be insured for a small extra premium. Personal liability is included in all policies. This provides cover against claims arising from injury to a third party caused by your pony. Most policies have an excess clause.

TRAILERS

Once a child regularly takes part in competitions, the question of whether to buy a trailer or horse-box will arise.

In the past, it was quite usual for young competitors to attend all the shows within a 12-mile radius of their homes without using a horse-box. Today however, motorways and busy roads have made hacking any distance a risky business. And it is unreasonable to expect a keenly competitive child to be content with the few shows which are close enough to be reached on horseback.

It may be possible to beg a lift from time to time in someone else's trailer, but friends, however obliging, may not always be going to the same event. Even if they are, your classes and theirs may not coincide. One or other of you will be kept hanging about, either having to arrive too early or leave too late. It is possible to hire a trailer, but sooner or later, you will probably decide to buy one.

Always buy the best trailer you can afford. Trailers range in size from those which can take two ponies, to those big enough for two 17.2 hh horses. Single-sized trailers are available, but most horses and ponies travel better with a companion, and to take someone else's pony in your trailer will add very little to the expense.

A trailer with a front-unload (that is, fitted with a front ramp as well as a rear one) is heavier than one with a rear ramp only. On the other hand, it is easier and safer to lead a horse forwards out of the trailer than to back him down a rear ramp. It is also easier to get a shy loader into a front-unload trailer.

The floor is particularly important as this is the part which is likely to rot. It should be made of hardwood, preferably with a 3 mm ($\frac{1}{8}$ in) gap between the planks so that urine can drain easily and air can circulate to speed up the drying. The lighting system should work properly; side and tail-lights, braking lights and indicators are operated from the towing vehicle. If possible have the wheel bearings examined.

A double-axle trailer is more stable than one with only a single axle. Inspect the tyres carefully, especially the tyre walls. Since a trailer often spends more time parked than in use, the tyre treads are likely to wear less quickly than the tyre walls.

Inside, most trailers have padding on the side walls and a central, removable partition, which may be no more than a single bar secured fore and aft by a vertical pillar. Partitions which reach to the floor should be padded. There are usually detachable breast bars and jockey straps.

Some trailers are fitted with non-slip matting on the ramps, which deadens the sound as the pony is being loaded.

Second-hand trailers are advertised regularly in magazines and local papers. If you buy a second-hand trailer, the points to look at are the condition of the floor; the state of the lighting system; the ease of raising and lowering the ramps; the brakes and wheels. If possible, have the trailer examined by an expert before buying it.

TOWING VEHICLES

Most trailers can be towed quite easily by a family car with an engine capacity of 2,000 cc. A tow-bar will be needed on the car. Four-wheel drive vehicles are at an advantage in wet weather conditions.

TOWING A TRAILER

Of all the duties that a pony-owning parent is expected to fulfil, to tow a trailer with horses inside is the one which causes the most apprehension. Yet many do so regularly without mishap.

If you have never towed a trailer before, start by taking it out on the road when it is empty. An empty trailer is not exactly like a full one, but it will give you an idea of how your car behaves with a trailer behind it and you can practise starting, stopping, and turning corners without having to worry about any passengers.

Practise reversing as well. This can cause all sorts of difficulties, so it is wise to master the technique as soon as possible. It may help to have a look at the way a toy Land-Rover and trailer work, provided the toy has movable front wheels operated by the steering wheel. It will show you exactly what the trailer does when you steer the towing vehicle. The trailer acts in an opposite fashion to the car. In other words, if you wish the trailer to bend to the right, you turn the car's steering wheel to the left, reversing the wheel only when the movement has been established. Try it out a few times with the toy trailer on the carpet.

Once on the road with a loaded trailer, you should aim to give the occupants as smooth a ride as possible. This means early anticipation of changes of direction and speed. Remember that your stopping distances are increased by the weight of the trailer, and start changing to a lower gear well before you reach a road junction so that you can come to a stop without any unnecessary jerk. You should also move off as smoothly as possible, taking time to go through the gears.

Take corners slightly wider than you would if you were driving the car by itself, to allow for the extra width of the trailers, and at crossroads bear in mind the extra length of car and trailer combined.

If you are taking only one horse or pony in a double trailer, the animal will have a better journey if he is loaded into the right-hand side. With two ponies of different sizes, travel with the bigger one on the outside.

The speed at which you travel depends on the nature of the road. Although 50 mph (80 km/h) is the legal limit, it is better to keep the speed to a maximum of 40 mph (64 km/h). The time lost on a journey of 10 miles (16 km) is only a few minutes, and it is better to set off early and arrive with a pair of calm ponies, than to drive as fast as possible thereby flustering the ponies.

Finally, remember other road-users. There is nothing more frustrating for other drivers than to be stuck behind a trailer with no hope of passing it safely. So if you are on a narrow road and the traffic behind you is building up, pull into a lay-by when you see one and allow the cars to pass. You will waste only a minute or two at the most, but you will be making a worthwhile contribution to road safety.

LOADING AND UNLOADING A PONY

A horse or pony which walks quietly into a trailer first time, with no fuss, is a joy to own. Most ponies load quite willingly, but there are always a few who, through sheer naughtiness, like to make a fuss.

If this is the case with your horse, and as long as you are satisfied that the animal is not frightened, you have to be firm. Often, just the production of a lunge-line or whip will do the trick. A lunge-line is connected to one side of the trailer ramp, brought round to the other side behind the horse and gradually tightened around his hindquarters. Coupled with a firm leader at the animal's head, the extra pressure should be sufficient to persuade him to enter the trailer.

If this fails because the horse swings his rear end off the trailer ramp, you will need extra help. Two lunge-lines crossed behind his quarters, with a strong person on each end, may provide the necessary compulsion. A further line, clipped to his headcollar and passing through a ring inside the trailer at the front, with the free end coming back out of the trailer alongside the horse, where a third assistant can apply steady pressure, is the next method to try.

Sometimes a horse just likes to take his time. If he likes to stand still and take a look around between each step, you will have to allow him to do this. Any sign of impatience will build up his resistance, whereas left to himself, he will probably walk quietly into the trailer eventually. You will just have to allow as much time as is needed before each journey. Greedy animals may be tempted into a trailer by the offer of food; other horses will load only if their companion has entered first. In every case, get to know your horse in order to find the best way of tackling any problem.

If your trailer has a front ramp it is quite simple to unload the horse. The handler gets into the trailer and removes the front bar. As soon as she is ready, the assistant outside lowers the ramp and the pony is led forwards from the trailer. When lowering the ramp, stand slightly to one side to avoid being knocked down or injured if the pony decides to make his exit at a run.

Unloading backwards is slightly more hazardous, as the jockey strap under the horse's hindquarters cannot be undone until the ramp is down. If a horse always rushes out very quickly, it is best not to use the jockey strap at all.

The handler should always talk to the horse in a soothing way, whether the animal is being unloaded frontwards or backwards.

PARTING WITH A PONY

At various stages through your child's riding career, you will be faced with the distress caused by parting with a much-loved pony. It is best if the old pony goes while the child is at school. There is bound to be a certain amount of grief, but excitement over the replacement will soon ease the pain. The process is easier when you already have a new pony to take the place of the previous one.

However, the main concern at this time is the question of finding a good home for the pony. If you can inspect his new premises and meet the family of the new owner, your fears should be allayed. But, of course, once you have actually accepted a cheque for the pony, he is no longer your responsibility. You cannot object because his new way of life is different from the one he had with you. However, if you discover that he is being ill-treated, you should contact the police or an animal welfare organization.

Many people decide to put a much-loved pony out on loan. With a little forethought, this type of transaction can be very successful. The advantage is that you still retain some control over the pony; and if the new home proves successful the loan might eventually lead to a sale. However, do make certain that your loan agreement covers every contingency, and that both parties fully understand what they have agreed to verbally. It is best to put all the conditions of the loan down in writing and to prepare two copies of the agreement, which are then signed by both parties.

Points to settle are the length of the loan; whether the loan is to include tack and other equipment; who is to be responsible for insuring the pony; paying for his feed, shoeing and veterinary bills. Discuss who makes the decision if, for any reason, the pony has to be humanely destroyed. If you trust the other family, it is better to leave this to them; a pony should not have to suffer unnecessarily because you are away when the decision has to be made.

A PARENT'S INVOLVEMENT

It is inevitable that your child's interest in riding will involve you increasingly as she gets older, even if you have no previous experience of horses. Many parents find that their lives and leisure take on a new dimension when their children take to riding. There are so many ways in which parents can become involved; supervising the care of the pony, driving to and from shows, building show-jumps for the paddock at home, and helping in the organization of the local branch of the Pony Club. Some parents dread the day that their children finally give up riding, but the Pony Club does provide them with the opportunity for continued involvement with horses long after their children have grown up.

APPENDIX I

The Pony Club

All young riders, whatever their ability, are well advised to join the Pony Club. This is an organization for children and teenagers, up to the age of twenty-one. It has helped and encouraged many thousands of young pony riders, including many well-known riders who have reached the top of their profession.

The Pony Club was formed in 1929 in the UK, where there are more than 350 branches, with a further 1,500 branches or affiliated clubs in other parts of the world.

Each branch is run by voluntary helpers, headed by a District Commissioner, and organizes a variety of riding activities, both instructional and competitive. These include working rallies, where instruction is given according to a rider's ability; competitions with neighbouring branches; outings to major horse shows; and other activities such as scavenger hunts, quizzes, barbecues and discos.

Most branches run an annual camp where, in addition to learning about pony care and management, members have the chance to train in various competitive forms of riding, such as show-jumping, gymkhana games, cross-country and dressage. Some branches also run teams for specialized events such as tetrathlon (riding, running, swimming and shooting) and polo.

All instruction at working rallies and camps is given by trained instructors. To ensure that good riding standards are maintained, members may take tests, the easiest of which is the D test, and the hardest the A test. Very few reach the latter standard, and those who do usually go on to a career with horses.

The annual subscription is not high, and all young riders derive some benefit from membership, if only the opportunity to make friends among people with the same interests. It also provides access to adults with experience and knowledge of ponies and horses, whose advice you will almost certainly need from time to time.

If you do not know who runs the Pony Club in your area, you should write to the national headquarters (see Address List), who will be able to give you the name and address of your nearest branch.

APPENDIX II
Address list

Britain

Association of British Riding Schools
Chesham House
56 Green End Road
Sawtry
Huntingdon
Cambridgeshire PE17 5UY

British Horse Society *and*
British Show Jumping Association *and*
The Pony Club
British Equestrian Centre
Kenilworth
Warwickshire CV8 2LR

British Show Pony Society
The Croft House
East Road
Oundle
Peterborough
Northamptonshire

Byeways and Bridleways Trust
9 Queen Anne's Gate
Westminster
London SW1

English Riding Holidays and
Trekking Association
Homestead Farm
Charlton Musgrave
Wincanton
Somerset

Horse Rangers Association
The Royal Mews
Hampton Court Palace
East Molesey
Surrey

International League for the Protection
of Horses
67a Camden High Street
London NW1

Irish Horse Board
St Maelruans
Tallaght
County Dublin
Ireland

National Pony Society
Cross-and-Pillory Lane
Alton
Hampshire

Ponies of Britain
Ascot Racecourse
Berkshire

The Pony Club
British Equestrian Centre
Kenilworth
Warwickshire CV8 2LR

Riding for the Disabled Association
Avenue R
National Agricultural Centre
Kenilworth
Warwickshire CV8 2LZ

United States

American Association of Sheriff Posses and
Riding Clubs
8133-B White Settlement Road
Fort Worth
TX 76108

American Horse Council
1700 K Street NW
Washington
DC 20006

American Horse Protection Association
1312 18th Street NW
Washinggton
DC 20036

American Horse Shows Association
598 Madison Avenue
New York
NY 10022

Pony of the Americas Club Inc
PO Box 1447
Mason City
IA 50401

United States Pony Clubs
303 High Street
West Chester
PA 19380

Canada
Canadian Equestrian Federation
333 River Road
Vanier
ON K1L 8B9

Canadian Pony Society
387 Hay Street
Woodstock
ON N4S 2C5

Australia
Australian Riding Pony Association
Seymour Road
Nar Nar Goon
Victoria

Pony Clubs Association of Western Australia
13 Violet Gardens
Shenton Park
WA 6008

South Australia Horse Society
Fisher Road
Hahndorf
SA 5245

Western Australia Horsemen's Association
50 Bombard Street
Mount Pleasant
WA 6153

South Africa
South African National Equestrian Federation
PO Box 52365
Saxonwold 2132

Index

Page numbers in *italics* refer to illustrations.